Lydia Richter

The Beloved Käthe-Kruse-Dolls

Yesterday and Today

To Helene,

with a thousand best

wishes Yours Andrea

8/10/1993

Published By  HOBBY HOUSE PRESS, INC.
Cumberland, Maryland 21502

Thoughts on my Mother's Hundredth's Birthday

Beloved Käthchen!

I have been to Aidling: I have walked the path through the hilly meadows filled with delicate flowers. the valley below me. the lake surrounded by the mountain ridge. above me an endless sky with ever changing clouds. gathering to new shapes and floating apart again. The young leaves. the lambs. the mooing of the cows. the sound of churchbells ringing: all this as familiar to you as to me. How many times have we walked there together:

> "Whether wind blows in spring. or summer. or fall.
> whether flowers in blossom — all silence will end..."

We walked many a path together. the long and the beautiful. the difficult: in happiness and sorrow. in hope and in grief — in harmony. yet sometimes forlorn. — Now that I am to write a few words for this book. which deals once again with your dolls. or rather just these dolls. of their manufacture and origin: and which may also ask questions about the reasons and riddles. why your dolls are so unique. I feel a shadow of sadness. Because you. Käthe. the human being. are covered and nearly smothered by these same dolls! Because you yourself came into this world as a small naked bundle and you did not have. after all. a good start. no fairy godmother at your cradle. Your mother must have been a skilled seamstress because with that sewing needle she earned a good education for you. later on acting lessons. to finally release you at the age of seventeen into that city of sin. Berlin. where your first contract with the Lessing Theatre waited for you. meaning 250 Marks a month. "A fairytale jump". as you always expressed yourself. Yet it was nothing compared to the fairytale life at our Father's side.

What a change from your Mother's wretched sewing room into the free world of artists at the turn of the century. How life was throbbing in the "Café des Westens" in Berlin. the same people alwas gathering at the same tables. their great minds trying to tear the world apart or at least change it: young Gerhard Hauptmann. Max Reinhardt. Walter Leistikow. Gabriele Reuter. Ernst Mühsam. and of course Max Kruse!

You were blessed with the happiness of that legendary love which perceives the desire to give as a daily impulse: and from this desire to "just love" created the doll to be loved. the doll to be cared for. the doll as solace for a child's heartache — unaware in your spirit. without any commercial thoughts. And when we had to say our last farewell to you. Käthchen. there was no hidden whispering or grudge. only sadness and gratitude from unaccountable doll mothers. What a victory!

Sophie Rehbinder-Kruse

Käthe Kruse at the age of 80 with her three great-grandchildren, Dana, Oliver and Uwe.

Doll IH dressed in the national costume of Holland.

For the information, as well as for the historical documents, the author and the publisher would especially like to thank Mrs. Sofie Rehbinder-Kruse, Mrs. Johanna Adler-Kruse, Mr. Heinz Adler, managing director of Käthe-Kruse-Doll Ltd., Donauwörth, as well as Mrs. Biemann, Mrs. Kühn and Mrs. Vogelsang.

Author: Lydia Richter
Drafting, Layout, Text: Joachim F. Richter
Translation: Ursula Driskell, Michael T. Robertson
Photographic authenticity: All up-to-date colour photographs done by Lydia Richter, except for p. 3: Torsten Rehbinder; pages 28, 29, 30, 43, 72, 77 top, 83 top, 90, 92, 93, 96, 97: Joachim F. Richter; p. 98: Käthe Kruse; pages 99, 104, 105 below, 106 top, 108 below left: Sofie Rehbinder-Kruse; pages 71, 81: Hanne Adler-Kruse; pages 106 below, 109: Jochen Kruse; p. 89: A.C. Borgé; historical photographs in black and white: from the Kruse-Family archives; archive and factory photographs (prospectuses) from Käthe-Kruse-Doll Ltd.; Richter's private archives.

Contents

Doll IH as a boy in the national costume of Holland.

Homage to Käthe Kruse

Long before I turned to Käthe-Kruse-Dolls in order to explore their past, I was involved in collecting china head dolls and published books about them. But when asked which dolls I like most, with an honest heart I have to declare my love for Käthe-Kruse-Dolls. Of all the dolls manufactured in Germany today, for me even the newest of them leaving the Kruse-Workshops in Donauwörth are the most beautiful play dolls of our time. Nevertheless, I am all the more enchanted by the earlier Käthe-Kruse-Dolls; how can one explain the phenomena of love at first sight, how can one describe the fascination of these doll children? I am certain it is their simple grace and almost life-like naturalness which touches me innermost. Kruse-Dolls possess that certain something, they are so lovable that you feel the desire to put your arms around them, to hug and cuddle them.

Käthe Kruse discovered the ideal doll! Material and construction all played a necessary part to let the dolls become playthings; their beauty and radiation were the key to all children's hearts. Did the thought ever occur to Käthe Kruse that these children, as adults and mothers in later life, would rediscover their fondness for these dolls and collect them enthusiastically; while others, who were denied these enchanting dolls in their childhood, today forfeit some useful acquisition or pleasant enter-tainment in order to enjoy a genuine Käthe-Kruse-Doll or even a whole collection? Maybe this is the best present we as collectors and custodians of these little pieces of art can offer this unusual woman on her hundredth birthday. We not only relish in possessing our dolls – we restore them, we dress them (aiming at authentic clothes), we exhibit them at fairs and present them in magazines, calendars and books. These Käthe-Kruse-Dolls have enriched the world of children and adults alike. They have brought happiness and delight, well beyond the frontiers of our country, and made Käthe Kruse unforgettable. It is these small, lovable things that make our daily lives more beautiful. Käthe Kruse has to be thanked for this by all of us, big and small. It is in memory of her that this book was written and dedicated.

Lydia Richter

Käthe Kruse surrounded by her dolls, at the age of 70.

7

Käthe-Kruse-Dolls:
A Challenge to China Head Dolls

In 1910, with the appearance of the first Käthe-Kruse-Dolls, a new era began in the doll-world history. Being a mother, Käthe Kruse knew that a child could only love a doll as natural as the child itself. "A child for the child" was one of her mottos. This means not only a childlike doll's face but also the sort of material which feels soft and warm. She describes this quite strikingly in interviews for magazines: "My dolls are alive because they are little children which have to be loved. The secret of my dolls is the combination of simplicity, primitiveness and naturalness!"

So her dolls were carried by the spirit of a new philosophy influenced by the five years during which she had made dolls for her own children. In those days there was an abundance of china head dolls. From 1860 onwards they experienced a never expected boom lasting until around 1915. They started the industrial, mass manufactured play doll, achieving a production of several million pieces per year. Contrary to their immediate predecessor, the wax doll, which often had a flat nose, cracks, and an ugly face altogether caused by too much playing, china head dolls were charmingly graceful, sometimes of a glorified beauty. During the following decades they received perfection and were given turning heads, wigs, glass sleeping eyes, a movable tongue, a voice box saying Mama, jointed bodies with separate limbs, mechanical automation and much much more. Being weary of the all too sweet and lovely, in 1910 one additionally introduced the character doll lead by the so-called Kaiser baby from Kämmer & Reinhardt. Despite this consciousness of wanting to offer a child natural dolls as playing companions these were burdened by the same disadvantageous criteria as their brothers and sisters, the beautiful ones: their porcelain was unfortunately breakable, it was rigid and cold, the body joints squeaked and rattled. All these negative attributes were consistently avoided by Käthe Kruse when she developed a cloth doll which lent itself to every doll mother's loving cuddles and games just as much as it stood up to the emotional, rough and quite often punishing treatment offered by children. Her dolls were a real challenge to the china head dolls and their manufacturers.

Käthe-Kruse-Dolls:
Character Dolls?

The end of the five years, 1906 to 1910, in which Käthe Kruse made dolls for her own children and for everyday use, marks at the same time the beginning of a professional manufacturing of her realistic doll resembling the natural, life-like child. This corresponded to the idea of the so-called character doll or artist doll of that time. As mentioned before, in the same year 1910, the character doll was conceived with the appearance of the already mentioned Kaiser baby.

Parallel yet completely independant from Käthe Kruse, other artists worked on the realization of a life-like doll. To be mentioned is, first of all, Marion Kaulitz with her artist dolls. She introduced them for the first time in 1908 during the Munich Arts and Crafts Exhibition. They were celebrated as a new idea and stressed by the doll historian Max von Boehm as being individual and full of character, with an infant's grace. And yet they were too much of an art item and although they thrilled art experts as well as adults they did not interest the children for whom they were created. Marion Kaulitz was denied a great success. The First World War must have meant great financial trouble for her. We have a letter by Mrs. Lilli B. from Neubabelsberg written to Käthe Kruse on

December 29, 1915: "Dear Mrs. Kruse ... Everywhere, but really everywhere, I spot Käthe-Kruse-Dolls! I shall soon apply to you for the job of a partner. I bought three dolls of poor Kaulitz at Christmas time (Mrs. M. brought her to my attention). The poor soul had tried to commit suicide because of her suffering needs for another day's survival."

Further mention is deserved by Margarete Steiff, world famous for her Steiff animals. She introduced Steiff dolls made from felt material with soft stuffed bodies on the occasion of the Leipzig Fair in 1907. She also preferred a natural child's face but above all attracted great attention with her caricature dolls. They were funny to look at but did not at all meet the children's playing impulses as did Käthe-Kruse-Dolls. They were finally taken out of production and soon forgotten.

Whichever dolls may have stirred the toy market in those years, Käthe Kruse went her own way and created a new, very personal type of doll and an equally new method of manufacturing. Without even contemplating a commercial advantage or profit she discovered the ideal play doll through the hobby of making dolls.

In the doll school.

Two Dolls I on a postcard: "Mother's Happiness".

Käthe-Kruse-Postcard with Doll I: "Shopping Spree".

Human-like Dolls:
A Child for the Child

Right from the beginning, Käthe-Kruse-Dolls with their positive qualities were given strong publicity and attention, and these good write-ups added an important part to the fast success and breakthrough of her dolls. An inestimable help at the start because she did not have the means for expensive advertisements at her disposal. An article in the women's pages of the Berliner Tageblatt from September 19, 1939 dealt very late but all the more appropriately with china head dolls and the positive change of a toy called "doll", initiated by those Käthe-Kruse-Dolls. Summing up: "One day all that was changed. Käthe Kruse invented human-like dolls. First they were only seen in a few shop windows. One was amazed and could hardly explain why no human being had conceived this natural and obvious idea much earlier. Babys looking like real, small, but not always perfectly beautiful life-like children; bigger ones which one could actually hold without the risk of breaking them instantly. Käthe Kruse herself brought her great and ingenious idea to life. She let children participate in a movement which kept a whole generation of adults breathless: the struggle against wrong and lying; squaring up with kitsch once and for all. She made a start to a complete change in the judgement of toys for children."

The little People

"Whoever gives his child a doll as a present offers constant pleasure without disappointment because Käthe-Kruse-Dolls are made by hand in the best way and manufactured entirely of waterproof material. The little faces made of material are washable with water and a mild soap, with only rubbing to be avoided. So these artis- tically beautiful dolls are hygienically immaculate as well. They can be repaired at any time so that a child may spend his whole youth with it. Käthe-Kruse-Dolls meet an urgent requirement of our times." This advertising statement by the Kruse-Workshops is nearly sixty years old but characterizes suitably and convincingly what made this type of doll, made from material, world famous. This quotation, however, seems to be an understatement because it is restricted mainly to material and construction – restricted to the realization of a doll suitable for playing with. This is the principle which Käthe Kruse made her task in her experimental years between 1905 and 1910. The fact, however, that Käthe-Kruse-Dolls instantly conquered all children's hearts and almost logically their mothers' is nearly as important as their practicability. No wonder that one very often talks of these dolls as "little people" when one aims at describing and explaining their radiation and characteristics. At all times Käthe-Kruse-Dolls have been praised and esteemed as artistic products because they were and still are manufactured mostly in the manner of artistic handicraft. Whatever leaves the Kruse-Workshops after this thorough method of production today is still a doll with a high artistic standard. Quite rightly, for many years Käthe-Kruse-Dolls were referred to as artist dolls, for example in the toy catalogue by the firm of Niessner in Vienna from 1930.

This picture shows a pair of Dolls I produced before ▷
the First World War.

Familiensorgen.

Different Doll I arrangements on Käthe-Kruse-Postcards.

"The abandoned Husband" is the title of this beautiful postcard (scribbled in German: *"A Future Vision!? ha, ha, ha, ha!!"*

A Woman makes Doll-History

An Unpleasant Youth

Katharina Simon (Käthe Kruse's maiden name), was born in Breslau on Sept. 17, 1883, and wrote in her own words about her unhappy youth. She experienced the modest existence of the lower middleclass surrounding, the poverty of those years in a small appartment. Her loving and attentive mother supported her by sewing late into the night. She never experienced the precious family unity with her father. Her childhood and youth came to an end, when she left the girls intermediate school in Tauentzienstraße of Breslau. She wanted to become an actress. At the age of sixteen, she started with an aim of taking acting lessons from Otto Gerlach of the Breslauer Municipal Theatre. She had discovered her liking for the theatre a few years earlier when her Aunt Paula and Uncle Robert had taken her monthly with them to the Lobe-Theatre. She was so impressed by the performances of Gerhart Hauptmann, Strindberg and others, that her mind was already made up then.

After completing one and a half years of acting lessons, Otto Neumann-Hofer took her with him to Berlin, where she received a contract, with a considerable monthly wage of 250.– Marks, at the Lessing-Theatre. So, at the age of seventeen her career started as a permanently engaged actress. She brought her mother to Berlin, and took on the name of Hedda Somin as her stage-name. Very soon, she received demanding roles and invitations to act in Warsaw and Moskow.

Max Kruse Changes Her Life

Since sometime now, Berlin had become the Number One Art Center of Germany. A lot of famous artists and actors worked and lived here. One of these was a man called Max Kruse, born in 1854, who had, in his younger years, made a name for himself as a sculptor. In 1881, he was awarded

Two portrait studies of Käthe Kruse, at the age of 39 and 40.

the Gold Medallion for his "Siegesboten von Marathon". Among other things, his fame was based upon portrait busts of many artists, inventions and books. He was 47 years old, when he met Katharina Simon, alias Hedda Somin, who was only 19 at that time. As destiny would have it, two people were brought together, who respected art, and at the same time found a deep personal affection for one another. However, she explained to him that she would like to have children, but not get married. Thus, a modern partnership was developed, which later led to a marriage.

Mimerle and Fifi

Soon her wish to have children came to be fulfilled; on December 2nd, 1902, Maria was born; her pet name was Mimerle, which later was used to name a Käthe-Kruse-Doll.

Soon the second child was expected, and Max Kruse believed that the big city of Berlin was not the proper place for the development of mother and children. Meanwhile, he kept his studio in Berlin, and she was searching for a new home. From day to day, theoretical plans were being made as well as discarded for places like Paris, Vienna, London or Greece. At last, Switzerland became the desired country, so that Max Kruse brought his family to the Sanatorium in Oberwaid, where in 1904, their second daughter Sophie, nick-named Fifi, was born.

Ascona

After stopping over in Oberwaid, Ascona became the home for several years of Käthe Kruse and her two daughters. Here, nature was so beautiful and the world was so peaceful; here she was able to develop. She discovered painting, and with her first water colour paintings found great approval with her critical husband; she

wrote philosophical thoughts and enjoyed photographing. Max Kruse often came to visit them from Berlin, and so common outings were arranged. Her mother, who was brought to Berlin from Breslau, was also taken along to Switzerland. The clear mountain air of this area did the sick woman good, nevertheless she died in February of 1906.

The Potato Doll

The three year old Mimerle paid great attention, how her mother, day after day, took loving care of her sister Fifi. She wanted to do the same thing as her mother, and had wished for the coming Christmas of 1905 from her father "such a baby". Käthe Kruse (only after 1905 was she called this) wrote to him in Berlin about this, but he could not find anything which would suit his purpose. The porcelain dolls being sold seemed to him to be nothing for children, they were stiff, cold and hard, as well as breakable. Therefore, he suggested to her, that she should make her own dolls. It was a challenge for her to prove her own artistry. This rather harsh order, "make your own dolls", was an interesting task for Käthe Kruse, and had changed her life in that she became a doll-maker – for the time being, only for her own children. Today, what we identify as a Käthe-Kruse-Doll, then seemed to be a long way off. Her first doll was produced from a towel, filled in the centre with hot sand, knotted at the corners to produce the arms and legs, and then on the longer edge a potato was inserted and fastened. This was the head, whose eyes, nose and mouth were drawn on using burnt matches. Käthe Kruse reports that her daughter Mimerle loved this doll, and noticed especially that it was the weight, the dangling arms and legs which had made a real impression. It was these attributes, which many years later, would become of great importance for the production of "Träumerchen" (Little Dreamer) the so-called Sandbaby. Mimerle with her potato doll became the first "Käthe-Kruse-Doll mother".

From One Doll to Another

The doll mentioned above had only been a short time project, because the potato had withered, the sand had started to flow out of the temporary body and the shape of the head and body was not pleasing to the eye anymore. Soon, something new and sturdy had to be produced, because the two year old Fifi wanted to play with a doll just like her sister. Käthe Kruse used *muslin* for the body and for the head she used a plaster cast from the blessed Christ Child by Verocchio. Sewn together and filled with sawdust, Fifi's beloved Oskar was born. Soon, however, the sawdust started to trickle through the seams and cracks, so that the doll was a victim of the process of wear and tear.

The children kept on wanting new dolls for their birthdays as well as for other festive occasions, so she kept on trying to produce better, durable and more lovelier dolls. The nose caused her the biggest problem in perfecting these homemade dolls, but evidence of progress was obvious.

Nomadic Life came to an End

After living in Ascona for several years, Käthe Kruse lived a short time in Neukirchen, where in June of 1909 her third daughter Johanna, nicknamed Hannerle or Hanne, was born. Then from 1909 till 1910, Munich and Hiddensee were intermediate stops, before Max Kruse's wish finally came true that the whole family was united. At last, after 5 years they were together in Berlin. The Kruse family moved into a third floor apartment of the Künstlerhaus (Artists home) in the Fasanenstraße, where Max Kruse's studio had been located for many years. It was here that Käthe Kruse continued her experiments in making dolls, and this news spread quickly throughout Berlin's society.

The Great Event

A Fiamingo head which was acquired in Munich, was the further stepping stone in the course of her experiments. Käthe Kruse used this head as a model and produced (with the help of wax and cloth) many heads which she then painted. Even though these dolls were imperfect, they were a further step towards the later Käthe-Kruse-Doll. In that same year of 1910, Käthe Kruse was invited by Herman Tietz Department Store (HERTIE) in Berlin to attend an exhibition of "Homemade Toys", and to take part in it. Obviously they thought that she would display the dolls she had made for her daughters. This would not have been a good idea, because having been played with, they had certain blemishes.

Therefore, new dolls had to be produced, and once again the nose proved to be a great problem. In her own words Käthe Kruse had written that Max Kruse "had stepped down from his high Throne of Art to help me solve my smaller problems".

The embodied result of working together was presented at the exhibition for "Home-made Toys". The Käthe-Kruse-Doll was born! It was admired and closely looked at by all. Newspaper and magazine articles were full of praise relating to the unbreakable, washable cloth dolls with their extremely natural and childlike expression.

Commercial Interest

To her own surprise, many enchanted mothers came to her Berlin apartment to ask her if she would make some dolls for their children. This was not the only commercial interest, which was aroused. The newspaper reports about the exhibition "Home-made Toys", awakened interest with traders and manufacturers of toys and dolls. Suddenly they all began to take great interest in this new doll, but were disappointed when they noticed that the eyes were painted and they did not have the popular sleeping glass eyes. The same was true of the painted hair; everyone was already used to the soft, human-hair wigs on porcelain doll heads. In addition, Käthe Kruse dispensed with using ball joints. Also, the head was firmly sewn on and not movable, this displeased the serious onlookers tremendously. However, everyone felt that something different had been discovered here, and that a new generation of dolls – a new philosophy would change the horizon.

Käthe Kruse, however, remained unmoved by so many suggestions, because the way she had made her doll, satisfied her imagination the most.

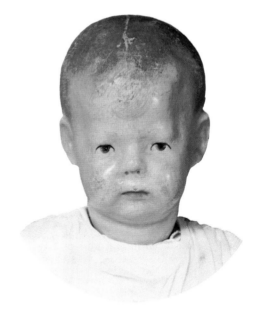

This Doll I produced under licence by Kämmer & Reinhardt in 1911 is a rare sample.

Kämmer & Reinhardt Produced the First Factory-made Käthe-Kruse-Doll

The business interest in her dolls had changed Käthe Kruse's life overnight, because she did not want anyone stealing the fruits of her work and experience. Therefore, she decided that her dolls should be offered to the public. The question arose how she should do this, since she did not have her own workshop. The nearest possible thing was done, in that talks about taking over the production were conducted with one of the largest manufacturers in the doll industry. At last, in December 1910, a contract was signed with this well known doll manufacturing company Kämmer & Reinhardt in Thüringia. Specialists were sent to Käthe Kruse in Berlin, so that they could learn the technique of producing the head and body; this was a difficult process of learning.

Even though, the workers of Kämmer & Reinhardt had learnt a great deal, the dolls which were produced were not to Käthe Kruse's liking. Also, the market was not satisfied with these dolls, because they could not stand upright; had a wide, floundery body as well as blue painted eyes. This was followed up with lively correspondence between Kämmer & Reinhardt and her, which also had no success. The contract, which had been signed prior, was dissolved, the rights to the dolls were transferred back to Käthe Kruse, and she repaid the 5000 Marks, which she had received as royalty when the contract was signed.

Therefore, in 1911, Käthe-Kruse-Dolls were only manufactured for a couple of months by Kämmer & Reinhardt. No wonder, that such dolls are rarely found. How they are recognised will be discussed later in the book.

19

America brought the Change

The attempt to produce Käthe-Kruse-Dolls with a manufacturer failed, and the future seemed bleak. It was in this situation, when in Autumn of 1911, the great turn-about came: a telegram from America landed upon the desk, for an order of 150 Käthe-Kruse-Dolls, which were to be delivered by November 8, 1911. Käthe Kruse was determined to fulfill this order, and produce the dolls herself. The race against time began, the apartment in the Fasanenstraße was converted into a doll workshop. Her helpers worked day and night sewing and stuffing the doll bodies. Max Kruse was forced against his own free will into making doll heads, she pressed into his hands a model and material, till he had produced so many heads, that he became the central figure for the production of the first Käthe-Kruse-Dolls.

At last the 150 "Americans" could be shipped off. The first consignment of genuine Käthe-Kruse-Dolls were on their way across the Atlantic to the New World. How many good feelings from Käthe Kruse accompanied them? Totally exhausted, she was able to relax; maybe she had realized that this spadework was to become one of the nicest occasions in her life.

A Further 500 Dolls

It was a great beginning, delivering the dolls to America, but an awkward situation arose. It happened, as Fifi and Mimerle were washing one of these new dolls, that the eyes were washed off. Käthe Kruse had stared in horror and thought about the dolls being delivered to America. Upset, she asked her helper, who had painted the eyes, what had happened; he confessed, that while working, he had run out of oil-colours and that he had used tempera colours. He believed that they would hold, because the heads were varnished. It meant that only a part of the consignment delivered to America were faulty, and that the promise "washable" was only partly true. One day, the buyer for the American importer came to Berlin, he was amused about Käthe Kruse's reaction, and had not come for a refund. Instead, he asked "If your dolls are really washable, would you please deliver another 500 to us!" She recalls later, that this was a great moment in her life as a young doll-maker and businesswoman; who had a bit of luck, which every hardworking person occasionally needs.

It has to be added, that her first son, her fourth child, called Michael was born in this eventful Winter of 1911.

One's Own Workshop ... somewhere!

After receiving this contract to produce another 500 dolls and to deliver them to America, Käthe Kruse decided at last to produce the dolls commercially. The production in the Berlin apartment was only temporary; apart from the helpers, there were five women and a painter, called Beyer, employed.

In 1912, the search began for a suitable workshop outside of Berlin. This situation was rather similar to the one in 1904, when she had moved to Ascona for a few years as a 21 year old woman. This time it was not as far: her new home had become Bad Kösen, near Naumburg a. d. Saale; where earlier, Max Kruse's mother had gone for treatment. This small spa was remembered for its healing salt-springs, where their daughter Hannerle had gone, when she had the whooping-cough. Bad Kösen became the new home of Käthe Kruse and her growing business. A complete floor of a villa in the Friedrichstraße was rented and converted into a workshop. Käthe-Kruse-Dolls and Bad Kösen now meant the same thing and from here they were

sent all over the world. In the winter of 1912, Bad Kösen became the birthplace of her fifth child, her son Jochen, nicknamed Jockerle.

One did get Married

In 1909, exactly 7 years after they had met for the first time, they got married. He was 55 and she was 26 years of age; they were together for 33 years, till he died. Käthe Kruse was the one, who had refused to marry. But, both changed their minds when one of their children had died at childbirth (Käthe Kruse had in all 8 children). If one were to believe an interview given by Käthe Kruse about Max Kruse, who was to have said: "We have to get married! If another son is born, we cannot have him being registered with the military as having no father!" However, being married, they were hardly together, because Max Kruse still kept his studio in Berlin, and she managed and took care of the fully equipped workshop in Bad Kösen, which could not have been moved without problems.

Pleasure in having a Domestic Life

The situation described above changed in 1915, when Max Kruse's sister, Anna, had died in Dresden, and he had inherited his parents' valuable furniture. A reason for him to show that he wanted to lead a normal family life at home. So, they discussed again, where their home should be. He felt that it should be nearer to Berlin, since Hannerle's whooping-cough was long gone; so they moved to Potsdam. They found an apartment to their liking, not too far from Sanssouci Palace. Everything was not completely perfect, because Käthe

Two historical pictures from 1911 showing child-like scenes with Doll I.

21

Kruse, who was bound by her work, had to commute between Potsdam and Bad Kösen. In the mean time, the First World War had left its scars, and the problem of getting food was great. So the Kruses decided to leave Potsdam, and from 1918 on, they lived together in Bad Kösen. It was here in 1918, shortly before the War ended, that a son was born; his name was Friedebald. He was used later as a model for doll number VIII, the "German Child". In 1921, another son, Max, nicknamed Maxlbaby, was born in Bad Kösen the last of her seven children.

The Patented Skeletal Body
The patriotic period of a militant emperor, Wilhelm II, led to a demand for soldier dolls by specialized dealers; so that in 1915, a "Small Soldier", approximately 10.5 cm (4 in) tall, was produced.

Max Kruse at the age of 48.

Described as the "Potsdamer Soldier", only a few of these realistic figures were ever brought onto the market. This doll was an important part of the history of Käthe-Kruse-Dolls. For its body, a wire skeleton was developed and fabricated, which made it possible that the arms, legs and body could be bent into natural, human body poses. This wire skeleton which was placed within this doll body, found use later within the doll house dolls, play dolls, "Schlenkerchen", "Träumerchen" and window-manikins; it was also used experimentally in cloth animals. This wire skeleton was invented by Max Kruse and patented at the German Patent Office on November 13, 1914, in his and his wife's name. The patent stated "... a model to be used to show at random different movements and positions of human or animal bodies ...".

Doll House Dolls
It will be news for many Käthe-Kruse-Doll friends, that between the period of 1916 and 1925, Käthe Kruse was occupied with making small figures for doll houses. They had well pronounced, modelled faces and heads. Her usage of elegant clothing made out of silk and other materials gave them an impression of being small works of art. For the body, a wire skeleton was used on the inside of the doll, as was found used in the "Small Soldier" (see above). Even the small hands had flexible fingers, so that they could hold, for example, a small cup from the doll house crockery, a walking stick or an umbrella. These approximately 14 and 19 cm (5½ and 7½ in) tall doll house dolls were brought onto the market in 1916 and left their mark on this type of doll. Käthe Kruse noticed that these dolls were mostly out of proportion. The heads of these small dolls were mainly modelled after portrait busts of relatives that her husband had made in earlier years. Due to

the fact that she had made them by hand and that they took sometime to make, the doll house dolls were rather expensive so that only a few appeared on the market. A great pity, since these dolls were a perfect work of art, "Artistic Dolls"; which could be made up into complete families, fairytale groups and show various different professions. They would have enlarged the selection of doll house dolls offered for sale.

Fakes

Käthe Kruse, like so many others, had to protect herself against people who copied her dolls. A prominent case known as the "Bing-Trial" in 1925, was awarded in her favour in the third stage by the Supreme Court of Leipzig.

The Supreme Court verdict is printed below: The demandress is the creator and producer of the "Käthe-Kruse-Dolls". The defendant B. had produced a large number of "Artist Dolls", and had them sold by the defendant N. The demandress complained that these cheap dolls were copies of her dolls. She appealed on behalf of the artistic copyright law under "§826 BGB" and "§1 UWG" that the defendants should not be allowed to continue selling these dolls, as well as to be sentenced for those dolls they had sold.
The court complied with the plaintiff's petition according to the artistic copyright law. The court of appeal rejected the petition. The demandress'es re-hearing had success. The claim was justified on grounds of dishonest competition (Law from June 7, 1909, §1). The Käthe-Kruse-Dolls with the same length and style (43 cm/40¹/₃ in) were produced from muslin. The head, which was copied from the Fiamingo head, was moulded. Through production there are differences in the stuffing of the heads (wood-straw), the painting of the face and hair as well as different styles of clothing.

Rare Käthe-Kruse-Doll house doll in original silk clothing, 19 cm (1¹/₂ in) produced in 1916.

The defendant B. produced cloth-dolls as well. The production of the head, as well as the clothing of the dolls, were the same. The only difference was that they produced four different sizes compared with the demandress'es-one, each with some centimeters difference.
Differences were found by the court of appeal. Especially the difference in head form. The dolls produced by B. were cheaper and detail was lacking compared with Käthe-Kruse-Dolls. Those persons who had no knowledge of these dolls, would not have seen the difference easily. This impression was inforced by the fact that these dolls had similar shapes, round faces and the same paint; the hair by both were painted; the nose, mouth and ears were similar; and the front part of the head was hard and the rear soft. Similar clothing

with both types of dolls made it easier to make a mistake when buying.

Käthe-Kruse-Dolls were longer on the market than B.'s dolls. Thus the court stated that this went beyond good moral ethics (RGZ vol. 73 p. 294, vol. 77 p. 431, vol. 79 p. 415, vol. 88 p. 183, vol. 92 p. 111; JW 1913 pf 1106 Nr. 7; "Leipz. Ztschr." vol. 20 p. 742 Nr. 16; Rosenthal, Wettbewerbsgesetz 5th Edition, Anm. 49f. to §1; Osterrieth in Gewerbl. Rechtsschutz 1917 p. 194; Kohler ebenda 1919 p. 1f.). Even though the defendants knew that they were deceiving, it was not necessary to determine this (RG II 31/20 from June 4, 1920 in vol. 64 p. 731). Due to the circumstances given, they accomplished an offence according to "§1 UWG". The court could have rejected this appeal. But they left the facts of dishonest competition unexamined. This is the case.

That is why court sentenced the defendants according to "§1 UWG", to stop producing and selling these dolls.

Thus the demandress won the case due to dishonest competition, and could have been granted legal protection of works of art according to the law of January 9, 1907.

A World Famous Article
from Bad Kösen

Käthe-Kruse-Dolls with their high, unchanged standard fulfill all of the requirements needed for a valuable trademark. The production was always controlled; especially the end control, by Käthe Kruse, and later by her daughter Sophie. Honours and prizes were the utmost symbol of recognition for the beauty and quality of her dolls. Thus in 1937, Käthe Kruse received a Gold Medal at the World Fair in Paris.

In later years approximately 12,000 dolls were made per year, using the traditional craftsmanship method of production. At the beginning of the War in 1939 the company had expanded to 120 people, made necessary by the production of window manikins. Years before, the rented rooms in the Friedrichstraße of Bad Kösen had become too small. So, in 1927 Käthe Kruse bought a large school building. From then on, her dolls were produced within her own four walls. Naturally, some of these dolls damaged by their doll-mothers found their way back to the factory they were produced in to be repaired.

After 1945?

In 1945, the area around Bad Kösen was occupied by the Russians. Under these conditions the company continued with their production. However, Max and Michael, both sons, contrary to Käthe Kruse and other members of the family, left for the West and became active: in 1946, Max started building up a new business in Bad Pyrmont, while Michael, in December of that year opened up a workshop in Donauwörth/Bavaria. In February 1949, both businesses were integrated. The second home for Kruse's-Workshop was to become Donauwörth, which to this day is still the home of the Kruse company. Since 1977, the business is fully owned by the family, after being in partnership with the Rhenish Rubber & Celluloid Factory (Schildkröt-Werke). In 1950, Käthe Kruse who was 67 years old came to West Germany, and took over the control of the company till 1956. In the spring time of 1955, she was there, as her newest child, the Turtle-Doll, "Model Käthe Kruse" was introduced at the Nürnberg Toy Fair. Her biggest wish at that time was to make her flexible window manikin popular. In connection with this, she held courses in Donauwörth for window-decorators, to show the practical possibilities of these figures. On occasions when she gave lectures, radio-, television-, and newspaper interviews, she radiated great vigour for

This is a fake Käthe-Kruse-Doll I, totally missing the radiation and charm of the original.

the pain as three of her precious family died one after the other within 3 years. Her beloved Max, companion, husband and close friend, who had influenced her life and success with the dolls, died in October 1942 at the age of 88. They both must have suffered, that his fame as an artist and sculptor had fallen into oblivion, and that her popularity kept on growing. Several years before her own death, she had said in a newspaper interview: "Is it not sad, that he would be referred to incidently in a newspaper article as 'My Husband', when I was his wife!" Thinking about his work, she continued with a bequest: "Do not forget my beloved Max!" Although his "Siegesbote von Marathon" had made him famous when he was young, he still appeared in public with a lot of his works. Max Kruse belonged to those pioneer artists of the 19th and the beginning of the 20th Century, which was reflected, for example, in his graphic sceneries for Max Reinhardt's Theatre, and in his portrait busts of Gerhart Hauptmann, Friedrich Nietzsche and others. He also invented a sculpture-reproduction-machine, whose movable arms could be used to reproduce a bust out of either wood or granite; enlarge or make it smaller. On November 8, 1894, the all-round artist and inventor handed in a patent application for the "Method of Perfecting Lithophanes", through which the two-dimensional lithophanes became three-dimensional, therefore plastic.

The next misfortune occurred several days before Käthe Kruse's 60th birthday, as on August 30, 1943, her son Jochen, or Jokkerle, died at the age of 32 in a military hospital in Berlin. He, just like many of his brothers and sisters, helped for a short time in the family business and was mainly occupied in decorating the window manikins, especially the artistic arrangements, as well as photographing them skilfully. Most of the Kruse-Workshop pictures

her age. Travelling to business friends in and out of the country was also one of her many activities.

She also spent many hours helping people who had written to her with problems. To help these people, gave her great pleasure.

A Suffering Period

Käthe Kruse, who was successful and well admired, was only human after all. She experienced the ups and downs of life and was a woman and mother who could suffer as well. She had just turned 25, as on April 4, 1908, her fourth child, a son named Johannes, was born dead. This pain was only suppressed due to the birth of her daughter Hannerle, 14 months later. She needed a far stronger heart to overcome

taken for prospectuses and catalogues from 1930 onwards were taken by him; he also worked as a decorator in Hamburg and had been an apprentice at Michel's Silkstore. Seven months after his death, on March 23, 1944, his brother, Käthe Kruse's son Friedebald, died in a tragic military accident. His young face had been immortalized in Doll VIII, which had been modelled after him. This so-called "German Child" had become the most successful Käthe-Kruse-Doll. So now, this promising life of a 26 year old had ended. He had passed his school-leaving examination in 1937 in Weimar and had wanted to become an architect. In the 1960's, at the end of a newspaper interview, the 80 year old Käthe Kruse had said: "Two of my seven children, two sons, died during the War. I will never be able to get over this. They were my boys."

Käthe Kruse also had a lot of happy moments with her children. In close connection to this, her daughter Mimerle needs to be mentioned. She had a certain close relationship with her father, whom she called "Herzlieb" (Heart-love) just like the rest of the family, from childhood on.

One has to imagine, that Max Kruse was already 70 years old, and that Mimerle was only 22 and ready for marriage. She took care of him, travelled with him, nursed him right up to his death in 1942 in Berlin.

She also devoted herself to her mother's last years. In the 1960's, she had lived with her mother in Munich, nursed her, and was loyal to her up to the end. Käthe Kruse died of heart seizure on July 10, 1968, at the hospital in Murnau/Oberbayern, just before completing her 85th year. Maria, "Mimerle", 80 years of age now, remained unmarried, and is living in Munich.

An original signed photograph from July 1958.

Not more than Five Types of Doll-Heads

The most important question, how many types of doll-heads were produced by Käthe Kruse, will now be explained fully. Many enthusiasts of Käthe-Kruse-Dolls believe that there were a great number of different doll-heads, because a lot of names and models were listed in company documents and prospectuses. One would come to the conclusion that there were many types of doll-heads. But also doll collectors, who know that the Doll XII, Hampelchen, is a charming doll, are misled in thinking that logically there must be 12

different types of doll-heads if the doll is given the number XII. Actually, between 1910 and 1956, only 5 different types of doll-heads were produced. From 1957 onwards, a new era began, as the first of three new types of doll-heads called "Model Hanne Kruse", extended the prospectus (see page 80).

On the following pages, the five historical types of doll-heads, from the period of 1910 to 1956, will be described in detail. To begin with their description:

Doll I: The first Käthe-Kruse-Doll had no individual name, and was simply called Doll I.
Doll II: "Schlenkerchen".
Doll V/VI: "Träumerchen" and "Du Mein".
Doll VIII: "Deutsches Kind", (German Child).
Doll XII: "Hampelchen".

Explanation:
Dolls with the numbers III, IV and XI did not exist. They were neither in the company prospectus, nor were they known in the Käthe-Kruse-Workshop or to the workers or to a third party. Maybe these dolls were only experimental ones, which were to get these numbers, but were never produced or sold on the market.

The Dolls V/VI have the same type of head, but "Träumerchen" had closed eyes and "Du Mein" had the open eyes. The Dolls VII, IX and X are the smaller copies of Dolls I and VIII (see page 28), so that from 1910 to 1956 exactly 5 types of doll-heads were produced.

Maria Kruse, nicknamed Mimerle, with her mother. Below: Doll house dolls enjoying a car-ride.

27

Doll I

This was the first and oldest Käthe-Kruse-Doll; and was simply called Doll I.

In 1910, Käthe Kruse after 5 years of experimenting was able to introduce to the public a cloth-doll at the exhibition for "Home-made Toys". This doll was produced up to the 1950's with very few changes.

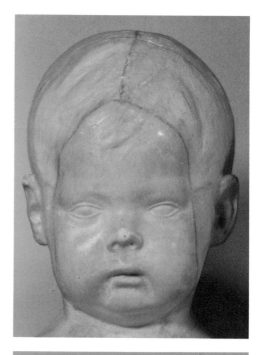

Doll I was entirely made out of cloth (muslin) by hand, was soft, warm, washable and unbreakable. In those days, this doll portrayed the beauty of a well fed 2 to 3 year old child with very wide hips. The styling of the body was rather complicated; 7 pieces of cloth were used for the torso and 5 pieces of cloth for the legs. The arms consisted of two pieces of cloth; the fingers were separately quilted and the thumbs were sewn on separately. Then, the arms were sewn on between the head and body, whereas the legs were attached by disc-joints. The head proved to be the biggest problem; a Fiamingo head with a classic beauty was the model and not, as is falsely suggested, a child of Käthe Kruse.

Using the technique developed by Max Kruse for the production of heads, pieces of cloth were cut, soaked in glue and stucco and were then pressed by hand into a bronze mould; after becoming solid, they were stuffed and sewn. To stuff the head and body, deer or reindeer hair was used, and at the very beginning wood wool.

The painting of the head, eyes and hair were done by hand using oil colours, which meant that the helpers had to be talented artists. In 1929, very few Dolls I had real

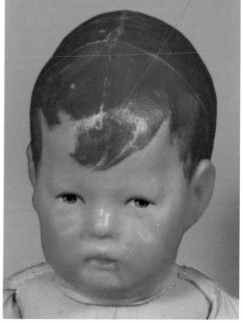

A unique document hitherto unpublished: the Fiamingo head from which the first Käthe-Kruse-Dolls were produced in 1910. The direct comparison of this Doll I shows the similarity. Many doll lovers are wrong in assuming that this successful doll was modelled after one of Käthe Kruse's children.

hair-wigs. From 1936 on, Dolls I were produced with wigs and were then called Doll IH. Each doll being hand painted, they were not similar; so, no one can say that all earlier Käthe-Kruse-Dolls ressembled each other. They were equipped with either a boy's or girl's wig, were dressed in either boy's or girl's clothes and were given corresponding names, so that they could be set apart in catalogues. Two famous names from the first catalogues were "Rotkäppchen" and "Deutscher Michel". The doll with the ball-joints (see page 31) (sought by many collectors) must have originated in 1911 from the period of cooperation with Kämmer & Reinhardt, because the daughter, Sophie, believes that Käthe Kruse never produced ball-joints herself. She was against having visible joints.

Signing: Real Käthe-Kruse-Dolls were stamped with the signature of Käthe Kruse and a number on the left foot, and a company tag was hung on them.

"Bambino"

"Bambino" doll, 22 cm (8³/₄ in), with a head from Doll I was produced as "the Doll for a Doll". At first, it was used as a decoration piece, but later on it came onto the market as a throw-around doll. It is seen quite often on postcards and other pictures together with Doll I; today however, this doll is hardly found. No one recalls which year this doll may have been produced, but it could be the period around 1915 to 1925.

Similar to Doll I, this "Bambino" has painted hair: the head, however, is not made from cloth but from a particular kind of plaster. This doll was not successful.

29

Two earlier Dolls I, the boy holding a Bambino-doll (described on page 29). On the right: In 1911, Käm-mer & Reinhardt had produced only for a couple of months this Doll I for Käthe Kruse. A distinguishing mark are the ball-jointed knees.

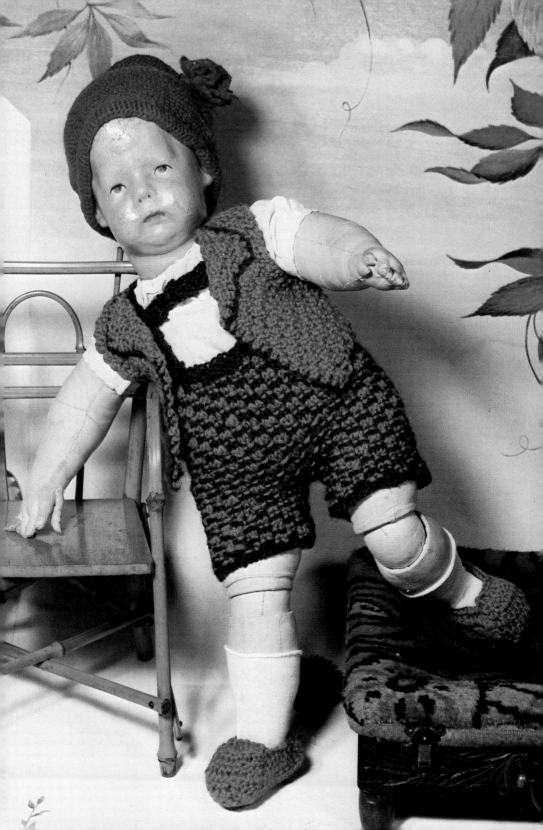

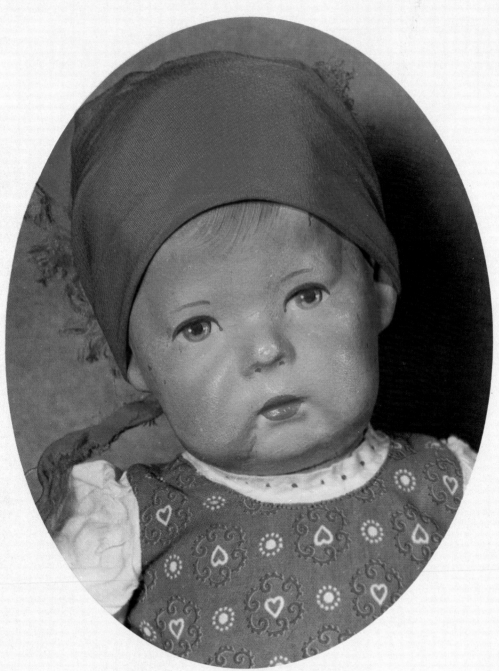

Portrait of a Doll I produced in the 1920s. On the right: a well-preserved Doll I from around 1928 with a Dutch cap. "Sternschnuppchen" (page 34), 35 cm (13³/₄ in), small version of Doll I, the bonnet sewn

onto the face mask, soft stuffed body. A rare prospectus (page 35), 1927, for which a special technique was to produce the colour photographs. Pages 36/37: Dolls I with hair (IH).

Die Käthe Kruse-Puppen sind ganz aus Stoff gefertigt,
auch der Kopf. Mit Wasser und Seife gut zu reinigen
(Reiben vermeiden). Die Reparaturwerkstätte ist das ganze
Jahr geöffnet.

Nur das sind Käthe Kruse-
Puppen, die auf der linken
Fußsohle den Namenszug
Käthe Kruse
tragen, und am Handgelenk
die Schutzmarke

Lauter kleine Käthe Kruses

LORLE	STERNCHEN	ANNELE	LOLA	ECKCHEN	SASA
Indanthren-druck.	Wollmousseline-Kleidchen		Indanthrendruck-Kleidchen		Lichtechter Voile.
Puppe VII A 24	Puppe VII C 28	Puppe VII C 26	Puppe VII B 30	Puppe VII A 23	Puppe VII D 29
M. 18.50	M. 21.—	M. 21.—	M. 19.50	M. 18.50	M. 23.—

Die bunte Reihe I

DANIELA	TESSA	STELLA	BEATE	GRISELDA	PIPPA
Voile mit Tüll-durchzug.	Wollstoff, plissiert.	Voile, Smokarbeit.	in Voile oder Seide.	heller Wollstoff mit Seidenband.	bestickter Voile.
Puppe I C 141	Puppe I D 154	Puppe I C 145	Puppe I D 151	Puppe I D 153	Puppe I C 144
M. 32.—	M. 35.—	M. 32.—	M. 35.—	M. 35.—	M. 32.—

Änderung der Stoffmuster vorbehalten.

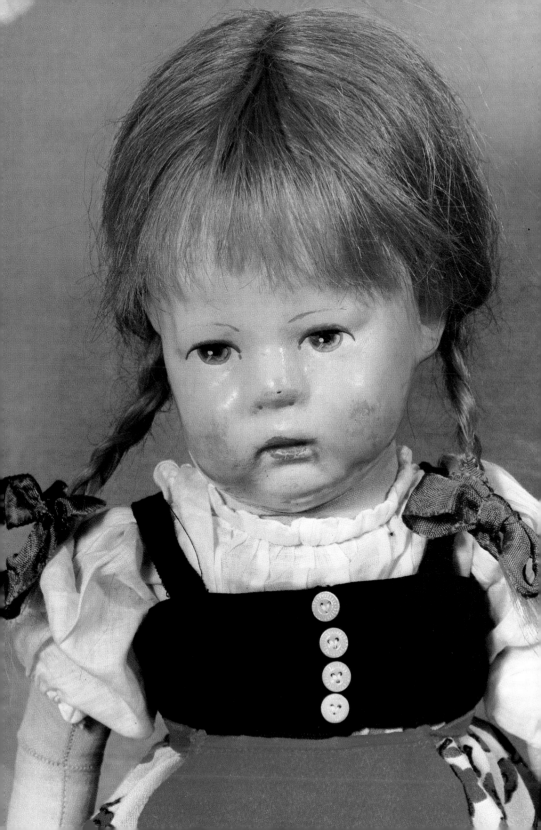

Doll II: "Schlenkerchen" (Little Floppy Doll)

In 1922, "Schlenkerchen", 33 cm (13 in), a cheerful doll was produced. His name was derived from his loosely sewn on legs, arms and head, which sort of dangled. His head, made from cloth, had a vertically running seam on the back of it, as well as painted hair, eyes and eyelashes; and was sewn on loosely. It was the only Käthe-Kruse-Doll who had a smiling, so-called open-closed mouth, whose lips were open but the mouth was closed to the rear. Till then, Käthe Kruse had tried to avoid giving her dolls a facial expression. They should neither laugh nor cry, so that a child should be given the opportunity of interpreting its own feelings into it. To this day, "Schlenkerchen" remains to be the only smiling Käthe-Kruse-Doll. Likewise, it was the only Käthe-Kruse-Doll with painted eyelashes and open eyes. "Träumerchen" has also painted eyelashes, but has closed eyes. Not until the 1960's did "Rumpumpel" (Model Hanne Kruse) have open eyes, sometimes painted with or without eyelashes.

The body of "Schlenkerchen" was produced with the firm's own method of craftsmanship. The child-like contours were modelled onto a metal skeleton using wadding and gauze, and then covered with the best kind of stockinet.

Consequently, the naked body was very soft and pliable, and was suitable for cuddling. A great pity, that the production of this lovely doll ceased in the 1930's.

Signing: as usual on the left foot with the signature and control number.

"Schlenkerchen", which was only available in a height of 33 cm (13 in), has a smiling face and a slightly opened mouth. For the first time, it came onto the market in 1922 and had loosely attached arms and legs. The picture on the next page shows the cloth texture very well.

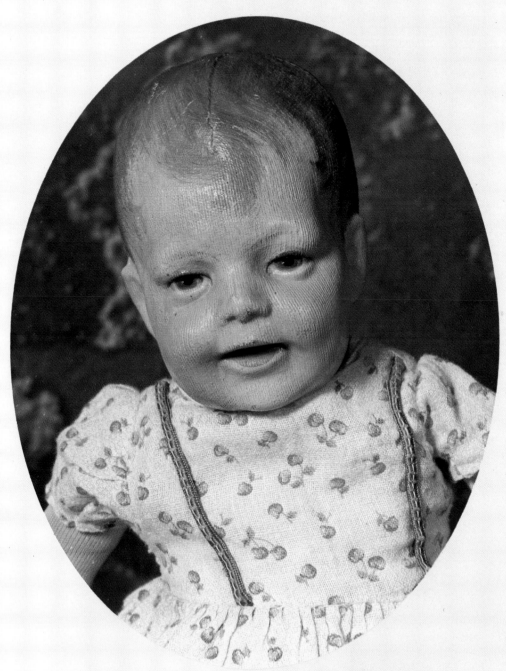

Extremely rare "Schlenkerchen" ("Little Floppy Doll"), Doll II, circa 1925.

From the book "Games and Sports" (out of print): six "Schlenkerchen" playing football.

A page from the prospectus of 1927 showing "Schlenkerchen" and "Du Mein". ▷

Puppe II und V
neue, kunsthandwerkliche Technik, ganz weich und
beweglich, ohne sichtbare Gelenke, auch nackt schön.

Puppe II, Das Schlenkerchen
33 cm groß.
als Hemdmatz M. 15.50

Puppe V w, Das „Du Mein"
50 cm groß,
als Hemdmatz M. 32.—

STRICKCHEN
aus No-Motta-Wolle,
ganz lid t.
Puppe II B 33 M. 21.50

Schlenkerchen-Puppe II

| MADI, II B 32 | LUCY, II C 29 | DER MAXEL, II A 1 | ADI, II C 30 | TROLL, II C 31 | | DER MAXEL |
| M. 21.50 | M. 23.50 | M. 19.50 | M. 23.50 | M. 23.50 | | M. 19.50 |

SCHUFTERLE
in elfenbein-
farbigem
Waschsamt,
handgebogt.
Puppe V w 26
M. 48.—

Du Mein, Puppe V

HANNEDANN V ... PUTZELL V ... DAUMELINCHEN V ... SCHNEEWEISSCHEN V ...

Doll V and VI:
"Träumerchen" and "Du Mein"

To prevent making mistakes, one has to remember that the terms Dolls V and VI were sold as "Träumerchen" with closed eyes as well as the "Du Mein" with open eyes. The same type of head was used for both dolls. To keep them apart when ordering, they were given letters at the end of each number:

Vs or VIs   = "Träumerchen", a doll with closed eyes;
Vw or VIw = "Du Mein", a doll with open eyes.

Dolls V and VI have the same head but differ in weight and size:

V = 50 cm ($19^5/_8$ in) and weighs 5 lbs,
VI = 60 cm ($23^5/_8$ in) and weighs 6 lbs.

Example and inspriration for this doll "Träumerchen" was the son Max, who was born in 1922. His head was not the model used for this doll. According to Mrs. Rehbinder-Kruse, this head was a copy of a baby's head mould, which at that time could be bought in any shop. The idea to produce a baby doll came from a doctor, who stood at the childbed of Käthe Kruse and suggested to her to produce something lovely like "Max-Baby" as a training-aid for young girls, instead of some horrible leather contraptions.
Around 1925, a life-size baby doll, 50 cm ($19^5/_8$ in) large and weighing 5 lbs, was created. The head was made out of cloth and was sewn on loosely, so that the head could sway to and fro, making it necessary to support it; the eyes were closed and painted. His soft and heavy body made completely from cloth was similar to that of "Schlenkerchen", except it was larger and heavier. The head and body were made heavier by using sand, hence the popular name "Sandbaby".
A little later, Käthe Kruse produced this baby doll in a different version with painted open eyes and gave it a lovely pet name "Du Mein". Both babies had painted hair, were produced either weighted or unweighted, and were offered with or without a belly button. Their sizes varied between 50 and 60 cm ($19^5/_8$ and $23^5/_8$ in) and their weight between 2 and 6 pounds. The sand weighted babies were used as training-aids, whilst the unweighted ones were conceived as play dolls. From 1930 onwards, the "Du Mein" was sold with a very fine hand-knotted wig, whose scalp – just like a real baby's – could be seen. Till 1940, the heads were mainly produced from cloth; running parallel to this since 1935, was the production of magnesit heads, a cement like substance. Around 1966, only synthetic doll heads were produced for this type of doll.
The body was produced in two versions: Type A) wound with stockinet, Type B) made from muslin and stuffed like all other dolls. For 10 years now, the body is made from formed foam-rubber covered with stockinet. In addition, the heads made out of cloth or magnesit, as well as arms and legs were sewn onto the type B doll, whereas they were cut in one with the torso of type A doll.

Above left: showing for the first time the original plaster head from which the "Träumerchen" head was produced (Doll V, the so-called "Sandbaby").

Below left: the same plaster head but with open eyes was used for the model "Du Mein".

The world-famous "Sandbaby"

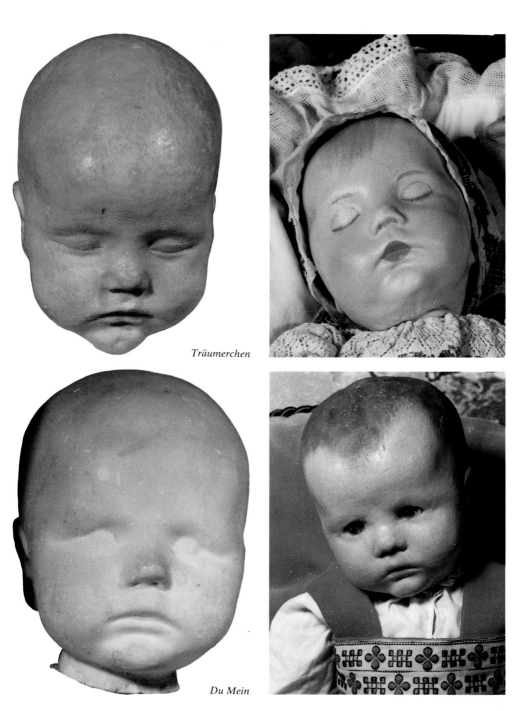

Träumerchen

Du Mein

Left: two cuddly old Kruse-Babies "Du Mein" and "Träumerchen" with cloth heads; right: a "Du Mein" with cloth head and wig.

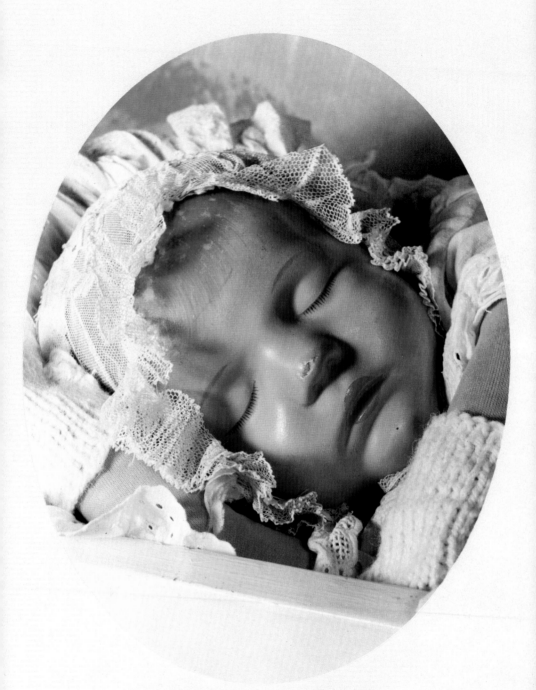

"Träumerchen", Doll VI, on both pictures having magnesit heads, left Doll V, circa 1935, right circa 1950 with sewn-on belly button.

Doll VII:
"The small, inexpensive Käthe-Kruse-Doll"

In 1927, due to the market, Doll VII, 35 cm (13³/₄ in), was produced. Two versions with the same size were offered:

First, there was Doll VII with the smaller cloth-head of Doll V/VI, the "Du Mein", with painted hair. From 1929 on, it was offered at request with a wig. Its body was produced with smaller proportions of Doll I, did not have so many seams, but did have its wide hips and the separately sewn on thumbs. Doll VII with the smaller head of the "Du Mein" is rarely found, because production was halted at the beginning of the 1930's. Incorrectly this doll is mistaken to be the first Käthe-Kruse-Doll.

The second version of Doll VII appeared at the same time in 1927, and was the smaller version of Doll I with painted hair, and at request was delivered with a wig. At first this Doll VII had wide hips and separately sewn on thumbs, but this changed in the early 1930's and it became slimmer just like the other dolls, and its thumbs were cut into the hand and were not sewn on separately. Contrary to the little Doll VII with the "Du Mein" head, this doll continued to be produced into the 1950's with a cloth head.

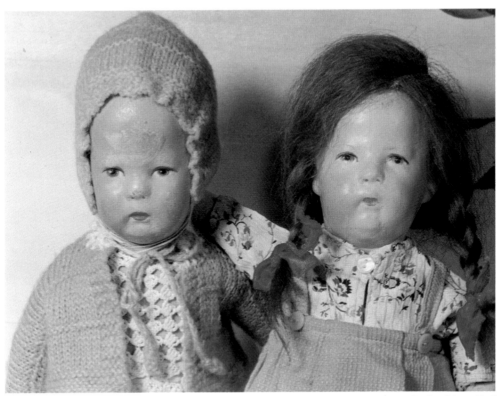

Two dolls Nr. VII with sewn-on heads (head type I); left with painted hair circa 1940, right with a real hair-wig 1929.

On the right: Doll VII with a smaller head from Doll Vw "Du Mein", sewn-on cloth head 1928. ▷

Doll VIII:
The "German Child"

In 1929, Doll VIII, 52 cm (20¹/₂ in) tall with the head modelled after Kruse's son Friedebald by Igor von Jakimow, had become a great success. He was the only child of Käthe Kruse, which a doll was ever modelled after. Friedebald's bust was reduced, and from this head a brass mould was made. The heads were produced by a simple method, the cut cloth pieces saturated with glue were not hand pressed anymore, but were produced by a flypress. The heads were not stuffed, but remained hollow, so by using a half-round wooden ball inside the head and a securing-pin, it was fastened to the body. This was the technical requirement needed for Doll VIII, the first Käthe-Kruse-Doll to have a turning head; and which had a vertically running seam in the middle of the back of the head.

The painting of the faces continued to be done effectively by hand; the hair of these dolls was not painted anymore. Sensationally new was, that the "German Child" was provided with a beautiful and expensive hand-knotted real hair-wig, which helped its success. The body of Doll VIII was not small and chubby like Doll I; but after simple styling, big and slender, which made it very attractive; the legs were fastened with a disc-joint. The "German Child" was also the only Kruse-Playdoll, which in the 1930's, was sometimes dressed in rather elegant and expensive clothes whilst usually one could speak of pretty and robust Kruse-clothes. As was customary, Doll VIII was offered in the catalogue as either boy or girl, depending upon its wig, clothes and name. The first pair of Doll VIII were named "Friedebald" and "Ilsebill". Käthe Kruse wrote that she managed to portray the magic of this child. Irritated, she later fought against the accusations made against the name of "Deutsches Kind"; although this doll came onto the market in 1929, four years before the Third Reich had been established. Historically it was prooved that Käthe Kruse

had an order to produce four 3-dimensional plastic sculptures of dolls, which should symbolize the European child: an Italian, a Spanish, an English and a German child, modelled after known portraits. From then on, at work, one spoke of the "German Child", and thus this name was used for Doll VIII (see page 56).

Two Dolls VIII, the most beloved pair "Friedebald" and "Ilsebill", 1929. On the right: an English Jubilee prospectus from 1936 with Dolls VIII.

Jubilee Prospect of the *Käthe Kruse* Dolls

Okt. 1936

Handed over by:

Für Kleidung nicht mehr maßgebend

25 Years Käthe Kruse Stuff Dolls —

throughout made by hand!

They were created for Mrs. Käthe Kruse's own children, and made on their features. The underlying principle was: they must be unbreakable (therefore they were throughout made by hand), they must be dear (for they are meant to be loved), they must be clean and noble work (so that the child can never feel disappointed somewhere). And there must be no mechanism in them, for love and mechanism cannot go together, for the little girl in her motherly feeling does not want to know, "how the doll is made", she wants to play and dream, and not be disturbed. And this has been the aim of these dolls: to educate the little girls for being motherly and loyal. Under this sign they have been victorious.

fig. 1 **Florrie in festive robe**
made of white dotted mull, long and wide, decorated with ruches and lace. The slip is made of silk cambric.

Doll VIII. "The Graceful Child"
21 in. high.

fig. 2 and 3 **Florian and Anny**
in light sportdress. Both in shorts, red and white belt, scarf, neck-tie, etc.

fig. 4 **Anny**
in light-grey sporting coat with lining, of soft wool, with a rock in the back. Fits all the dolls of series VIII.

fig. 5 **Tommy**   fig. 6 **Lillibeth**
in sailor's costume, in white or navy colour. White or navy caps with the inscription as requested.

fig. 7 **Tommy's**
sailor's coat fits all of them. Fine navy wool material, full lining. Anchor on the sleeve, golden buttons.

fig. 8 **Tommy**
in navy sailor's dress.

fig. 9 **Mabel**
in navy sailor's dress.

fig. 10 **Mary**
with two thick fair plaits, light-coloured washable dress and red little apron.

*"Das Deutsche Kind" ("The German Child") in fes-
tive clothing, left, cloth head from 1940 and right with
a synthetic head from 1958. On the right and following*
*double-pages (54/55): extremely well kept pair of Doll
VIII "Das Deutsche Kind" in original clothing; end of
the 1940s, finely painted, shiny irises.*

Models of doll "Das Deutsche Kind", 52 cm (20¹/₂ in), created for an exhibition from a painting by Julius Hübner; however, the small "Friedebald" head by Igor von Jakimow was used. Above right: The painting by Reynolds from 1928 was copied with Doll VIII, see below (Doll VIII see page 50).

Doll IX:
"The little German Child"

In the same year as Doll VIII was created, 1929, the Käthe-Kruse-Workshop in Bad Kösen produced a perfect copy of this doll, but in a smaller version. The "Small German Child" was manufactured in a size of 35 cm (13³/₄ in), therefore was cheaper to produce and could be bought by a wider range of buyers. Naturally, Doll IX, with the same head but different wigs, clothes and names was offered as either boy or girl. Just like her larger brother and sister, it became a great commercial success. These small Kruse-Dolls are extremely pretty and that is why, today, they are sought after by collectors. Also their heads, like Doll VIII, have a vertically running seam on the back of the head, hand-knotted real hair-wigs and a turning head.

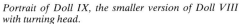

Portrait of Doll IX, the smaller version of Doll VIII with turning head.

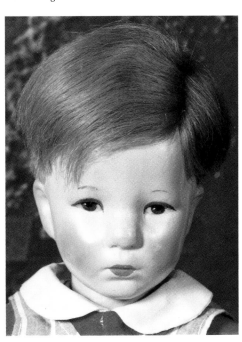

Picture above: "Ilsebill", below "Friedebald", both Dolls VIII. Star photographs from the 1930s.

The pictures on the following pages show clearly the great difference between Dolls VIII and IX.

Doll X:
The small Käthe-Kruse-Dolls

With Doll VII (see page 48), the firm had brought the smaller version of Doll I onto the market in 1927, and its stuffed head was sewn on just like Doll I. Now, this 35 cm (13³/₄ in) large doll with the smaller head of Doll I was to have a turning head, similar to the one made for Doll VIII.

Doll X with its moulded and turnable head came out around 1935.

Doll XII:
The "Hampelchen" (Little Jumping Doll)

"Hampelchen" which came out at the beginning of the 1930's, and whose name was chosen due to its loosely sewn on legs – with which it could prance around –, was made after a beautiful model of a child by Igor von Jakimow. Nobody can say to this day who was the model. On no account was it one of Kruse's children.

The cloth head, which was sewn on to the body, had three vertically running seams on the back of the head; a very important feature for collectors. Käthe Kruse wrote about Hampelchen, that it did not sell too well, even though, due to its loose legs, it could take on any natural pose. Maybe the mistake was that it could only stand with the help of a button and band on its back. Today this doll, because of its loose legs, is sometimes mistaken for Doll II, the smiling "Schlenkerchen", a popular and sought after collector's item.

Below are simple descriptions of various Hampelchen versions:

- Size 45 cm (17³/₄ in), with the head modelled by Igor von Jakimow, real hair-wig and loosely attached legs: this model appears the most; described as XII/H.

- Size 45 cm (17³/₄ in), with the head modelled by Igor von Jakimow; however, with painted hair; loosely attached legs; this model appears seldom; described as XII.

- Size 45 cm (17³/₄ in), with the head of Doll I or Doll VIII, mainly with painted hair; loosely attached legs; described as XII.

- Size 35 cm (13³/₄ in), with a smaller head of Doll I; mainly painted hair; described as XII.

- Size 40 cm (15³/₄ in), with the head of Doll I; painted hair or wig; loosely attached legs; late 1940's; name "the small Hampelschatz"; described as XII/B.

- Size 45 cm (17³/₄ in), 1951 onwards, with the body of Doll I, whose legs were connected with disc-joints; described as XII/I.

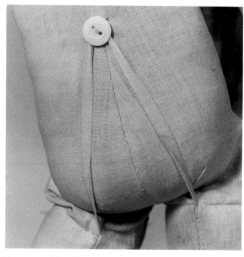

Button and band on the back helped "Hampelchen" ("Little Jumping Doll") to stand.

60

Two well preserved "Hampelchen"; (cloth) head by Igor von Jakimow, real hair-wig, 45 cm (17³/₄ in).

Doll XII "Hampelchen" with real hair-wig and cloth head after Igor von Jakimow.

Doll XII with painted hair and cloth head after Igor von Jakimow.

Collectors Guide: Ten Golden Rules for Historic Käthe-Kruse-Dolls from 1910 to 1955

The type of doll-heads, I to XII, described before are those whose head and body are made out of cloth. In the following, important distinguishing marks of real Käthe-Kruse-Dolls will be shown, so that collectors can educate themselves.

1. Markings

All real Käthe-Kruse-Dolls (with the exception of Turtle-Dolls) to 1955, had stamped on their left foot the original Käthe Kruse signature and a serial number, from which the age of the doll cannot be concluded, since this was a coded control number system. This stamp, in the meantime, is either worn or washed off. Furthermore, all dolls had a tag with Käthe Kruse's signature. These tags are very seldom found today.

After 1945 to around 1951, there was an additional stamp on the right foot saying "Made in Germany, US-Zone", and the same legend was found on the tag. After 1951, the same dolls were produced for several years in East-Germany. They have stamped on their right foot "VEB, Bad Kösen a.d. Saale", and on the left foot a triangle.

2. Sizes

For many years the size of Doll I, 43 cm (17 in), was a trademark for Käthe-Kruse-

Old tags with "Käthe Kruse" trademark.

Dolls, up to 1922, as Doll II, Schlenkerchen, with 33 cm (13 in) came onto the market, while Träumerchen and Du Mein, Dolls V/VI, were produced from 1925 onwards with sizes ranging between 50–60 cm ($19^5/_8$–$23^5/_8$ in). Dolls VII and X are the smaller versions of Doll I with a size of 35 cm ($13^3/_4$ in). Doll VII appeared in 1927, and Doll X was offered for the first time from 1935 on. The largest Käthe-Kruse-Doll number VIII, Das Deutsche Kind, came out in 1929 with a size of 52 cm ($20^1/_2$ in) and at the same time Doll IX, Das Kleine Deutsche Kind, with a size of 35 cm ($13^3/_4$ in). There are several versions of Doll XII, Hampelchen; sizes ranging from 35, 40, and 45 cm ($13^3/_4$, $15^3/_4$ and $17^3/_4$ in) (from 1956 to now, 47 cm [$18^1/_2$ in] tall). Additionally, in the 1940's, Doll I had been enlarged from 43 to 45 cm (17 to $17^3/_4$ in).

3. Cloth Head/Seams on the Back of the Head

The earlier Käthe-Kruse-Dolls had often a very thin coat of paint, so that the structure of the cloth was visible. If the cloth is not visible, one has to take a look at the back of the head. If there are three vertically running seams, like with Dolls I, VII, and XII, then one can be sure that it is a cloth-doll head. The cloth-heads of Dolls II, VIII, IX and X have only one vertically running seam, and Dolls V and VI can either have one or three vertically running

Stamp "Käthe Kruse" and number on the left foot.

seams. Also heads made out of cloth, whose under-base was card-board, count as a cloth-head and have a seam on the back of the head. This seam is sometimes so thickly coated with paint, that it is not visible. In this case, one should loosen the wig carefully from the back of the head. If it is a cloth-head the seam should be visible; if not, then one can be sure that it is a synthetic head from 1955 onwards. Up to 1928, all Käthe-Kruse-Dolls had loosely sewn on heads, except for those produced in 1911 by Kämmer & Reinhardt, who had turning heads and a seam on the back of it. The turning head was not produced until 1929, with Doll VIII.

4. Painted Hair
From 1910 to 1929, Käthe-Kruse-Dolls had painted hair: hence Dolls I, II, V/VI

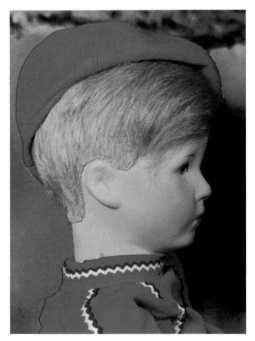

A beautiful profile of Doll VIII with a boy wig, well styled.

and VII. After this period Käthe-Kruse-Dolls received real hair-wigs, but still there were those with painted hair, for example Dolls I, V/VI, VII, X and XII; however, Dolls VIII and IX always had wigs.

5. Painted Eyes
With exception of the Turtle-Dolls "Model Käthe Kruse" with glass eyes, all Käthe-Kruse-Dolls had painted eyes. Träumerchen, Dolls V/VI, had closed eyes and painted eye-lashes. Schlenkerchen, Doll II, had open eyes and painted eye-lashes. The earlier dolls nearly always had shiny painted irises, but this can be found after 1940 on only a few.

6. Closed Mouth
Apart from Doll II, Schlenkerchen, with its open-closed mouth, all Käthe-Kruse-Dolls had closed mouths. The term "open-closed mouth", is taken from terminology used for china-head dolls. It means, that the lips are open, but the mouth is closed at the rear. The painting of the mouth, up into the 1950's, was characterized by the drawn through upper lip curve, which had no depth.

7. Body
Käthe-Kruse-Dolls all have sewn on arms, with exception of those produced by Kämmer & Reinhardt in 1911 with ball joints. The legs of Käthe-Kruse-Dolls numbered I, VII, VIII, IX, X and XII/I all have disc-joints; the legs of Schlenkerchen, Doll II, and Träumerchen, Doll V/VI, Model A) are cut in one with the torso, while Model B) and Hampelchen have loosely sewn on legs. To get the body to be life-like and to form the arms and legs well, the body-cut of Doll I consisted of many separate parts, which, due to the sturdy cloth, had to be sewn together using a fur sewing machine.

Thereupon, the torso and limbs were stuffed firmly with reindeer hair, which came from Lappland, then formed and modelled. Now the calves, thighs and hips of the compact and stocky Doll I appeared. Naturally, continuous progress through various different production methods, varied for each of these dolls.

8. Wide Hips

A very special distinguishing mark for old Dolls I, I/H and VII, was their wide hips, which were produced until 1930, but then became narrower.

9. Sewn on Thumbs

Apart from having an old cloth-head, painted hair and wide hips, Dolls I, I/H and VII, if they are from 1930, must have sewn on thumbs.

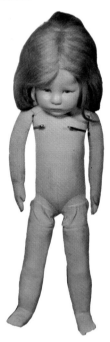

10. Arms

Apart from dolls made out of celluloid, all Käthe-Kruse-Dolls had sewn on arms.

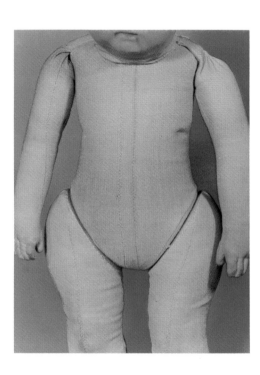

Besides the three vertically running seams and the extra sewn-on thumbs, the wide hips are the important feature of Doll I from 1930.

Left: The slim "Hampelchen", a body with loosely sewn-on arms and legs, model "Glückskind" ("Lucky Child").

The loosely sewn on legs of "Hampelchen" often lead collectors to errors. When collectors find a doll with such a body, they believe to have found the rare "Schlenkerchen", Doll II. The latter, however, is only 33 cm (13 in) tall and has a smiling face and a slightly opened mouth, a so-called open-closed mouth.

How to restore a Doll oneself?

With a lot of skill and love, a doll-collector restored this rather worn Käthe-Kruse-Doll. She only needed some water-soluble body colour and a very small amount of plasticine for the nose; in this case Fimo. By luck, the eyes were in good condition, for a novice with an unpracticed hand would find it difficult to paint them accurately. Several cracks had developed in the doll's face and head, due to hollow areas which had formed under the cloth, which in places could only be stuffed with some cotton. Since this model belongs to one of the earlier Doll I, the effort was rewarding. This doll cannot afford to be damaged any more.

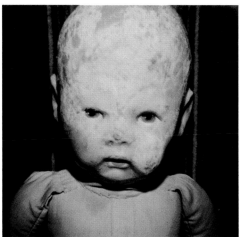

Badly damaged Doll I with missing point of the nose.

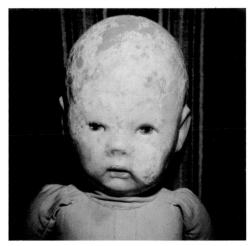

The point of the nose repaired with plastecine.

After restoring and painting the face.

The restored child ready for cuddling again.

Modern Times:
Old Types of Heads of Käthe-Kruse-Dolls after 1955

Heads made from Synthetics

At the beginning of the 1950's, the Kruse-Workshop found itself in a financial crisis, and one had to start thinking about reducing production costs. New ways and easier methods had to be found. So from 1952, they started experimenting, producing synthetic doll-heads. Since each new change had to be tried out and introduced, this meant, that the production of cloth dolls using the old method of the fly-press and moulding under high pressure continued to run parallel. Also, the magnesit heads were still produced at this time. (Magnesit is a cement like substance.) From 1955 onwards, many playing-doll-heads were made out of synthetics. Exclusively, the doll-heads V/VI (Träumerchen and Du Mein), which were mainly made for use in baby-care, were still made out of magnesit up to about 1965.

Painting and Wigs

The painting of the faces was still done by hand; the painting of the eyes was unchanged. The shiny irises were hardly painted anymore, and seldom found in the 1940's.

Worth mentioning is that the painting of the mouth in the 1950's lost its characteristic drawn through upper lip curve. From then on the lips were painted only with the heart-formed upper lip, which all other dolls had. The heads of Käthe-Kruse-Dolls were mainly equipped with wigs after 1955, painted hair was done seldom. As a rule hand-knotted real hair-wigs were used, but during the period 1953 to 1960, braided real hair-wigs were also used. From 1961 to 1976, in a period when real hair was expensive, most of the Käthe-Kruse-Dolls were equipped with hand-knotted synthetic hair-wigs. After 1976, only real hair-wigs were used. Mummelchen is the first and only Käthe-Kruse-Doll with a mohair-plush wig.

Regarding painted hair, one can sum up, that the Dolls 52H (known as the Deutsche Kind), Schummelchen and Flessibila were the only Käthe-Kruse-Dolls that never had painted hair, while all the other dolls heads were either painted or had wigs.

The doll bodies, above all, were produced after the old method from either muslin or stockinet and were hand stuffed with reindeer hair, or wrapped, but soon, in the middle of the 1950's, synthetics were used in the production.

As usual, the firm used the same doll head for either boy or girl doll; they just fitted its type with a wig, clothes, or name.

Signing

The signing remained the same until 1957; from 1958 onwards most of the dolls had the hand written signature stamped on their left foot, though the additional control number was dispensed with. Instead, from 1958 onwards, they started to imprint the date of production on the right foot. This date stamp was not used regularly; this has only been the case for the last 10 years. Each doll, in addition, received a tag.

Doll "47 H", with synthetic head, real hair-wig, 1983, ▷
the earlier "Hampelchen".

68

End of the old Names and Numbers

In the 1950's, the firm had stopped calling the produced Käthe-Kruse-Dolls by their customary names; for example Doll VIII (Das Deutsche Kind), Doll IX (Das Kleine Deutsche Kind), and Doll XII (Hampel-chen). Today, only Du Mein is still called by its old name in catalogues, while Träumerchen is not officially listed; in certain cases one can still order it. The other dolls of the old type were only named by their size and they had received additional letters like:

B for Babydoll
H for Hair
G for painted hair ...

So, for example Doll VIII (Das Deutsche Kind) was called simply Doll 52 cm H in the catalogues, and a few years later only 52 H.
The production of Doll II (Schlenkerchen) had already been stopped in the 1930's, and Dolls VII and X (the Little Käthe-Kruse-Dolls) at the beginning of the 1950's.
Collectors keep on asking what had happened to the first Käthe-Kruse-Dolls, for instance to the doll head of Doll I. After some inquiries the results were that this head (1956 to 1957) had continued to be produced for the doll Schummelchen and that from 1963 to 1968 for the doll Flessibila. For these, three different heads were offered. After 1968, this doll head number I ceased to be produced.

Description of the produced Dolls (Model Käthe Kruse) after 1950

Slim Grandchild ("Das schlanke Enkelkind")

For the fortieth anniversary, which was celebrated in 1952, a doll "Das schlanke Enkelkind" was produced. Its head (the Friedebald head) had a revolving neck and was still made out of cloth, later out of synthetics. This doll either wore a braided wig or a hand knotted wig; its body was made out of muslin and hand stuffed with reindeer hair; the legs were fastened by disc-joints. Since all parts of the body were very slim, as the name suggests, it was very difficult and tedious to stuff, so that they gave up producing this doll child in 1956. The signing varied, either left or right foot, with Käthe Kruse's signature, and vice-versa the corresponding number.

The earlier "Deutsche Kind" as it is presented today with a synthetic head as "Doll 52 H".

"Das schlanke Enkelkind" produced in 1952, 47 cm (18¹/₂ in), one with a short-haired wig and the other with plaits. ▷

Turtle-Doll "Model Käthe Kruse", made out of Celluloid/Tortulon/Demiflex

In order that an inexpensive Käthe-Kruse-Doll could be produced, Käthe Kruse decided to work with the Rhenish Rubber and Celluloid Company (Schildkröt-Werke), and to produce a Käthe-Kruse-Doll out of Tortulon; for instance Demiflex, a mixture of celluloid and synthetics. With this move, she had to become unfaithful to her principles of a warm and cuddly cloth doll. So, she gave her permission, for a licence-fee, that the Schildkröt Werk could copy and produce two dolls in the style of Käthe-Kruse-Dolls with the name Turtle-Dolls "Model Käthe Kruse".

From 1955 until around 1961, two different Turtle-models were produced with different clothing, hairstyles and sizes. A Turtle prospectus from 1961, offered among other things, fairy-tale dolls with the names Rotkäppchen (Red-riding Hood), Hans im Glück (Hans-in-Luck) as well as Hansel and Gretel. Turtle-Dolls (Model Käthe Kruse) could be bought in the following versions:

- with moulded and painted hair, as well as painted eyes or
- with moulded and painted hair, as well as glass eyes or
- with braided wig, made out of real or synthetic hair, as well as painted eyes or
- with braided wig made out of real or synthetic hair, as well as glass eyes, or
- with the head made from demiflex and sewn on wig, as well as sleeping-glass eyes, the latter according to the catalogue of 1961, had the names Monika, Susi, Gretel and Toni.

The painting of the heads was done by spraying the paint on, while eyes and mouth were done using templates. These doll bodies were all made out of synthetics; the arms and legs were fastened using rubber bands and metal hooks. Known sizes were 35, 40 and 45 cm (13³/₄, 15³/₄ and 17³/₄ in). These dolls were signed with a turtle and in addition with Model Käthe Kruse, and were only produced by the Schildkröt-Werke. The Turtle-Dolls "Model Käthe Kruse" were not successful, so that production ceased in 1961.

From 1955 onwards, most of the original heads of Käthe-Kruse-Dolls were made out of tortulon with real hair-wigs. Their cloth bodies were, as usual, hand stuffed, and the signing was found on the left foot. Since these dolls found no approval and the paint on their faces did not last, production ceased in 1958.

Left: the original Käthe-Kruse-Doll with celluloid head; right: a Schildkröt-doll, "Model Käthe Kruse", made completely out of celluloid.

A letter from 1955 in which Käthe Kruse explains the production of celluloid dolls.

Now here it is:

The new **Schildkröt-Doll** Model *Käthe Kruse*

and I know for a fact that my friends and followers will be in for a great surprise.

And one will ask me, "Did it have to be? Did not Käthe Kruse believe in a soft and cuddlesome doll? – Yes, and now after 40 years, she brings out a doll in her name, which is made out of a hard material".

I would like to answer all these understandable questions from the beginning. It is better to answer them once and for all.

Yes! I am and will remain a friend of the soft and cuddly doll, and I will continue to produce these soft Käthe-Kruse-Dolls in my company in Donauwörth.

Many have often asked me, "Make your dolls cheaper – can't you produce your dolls cheaper?". I received so much mail where these questions are raised that I always have to say, "No, I can't produce these dolls, made by hand out of cloth, cheaper; and that is why they will remain unbought by a larger consumer market and for an unaccountable number of little girls, who would like to have them. A great pity: –".

These unaccountable number of small girls should have their own Käthe-Kruse-Dolls. And if the parents find that my original doll is too expensive, then a cheaper method of production should be found, that still includes the beauty of the Käthe-Kruse-Doll, and having this special expression.

And so, you see how this idea was born. To produce the Käthe-Kruse-Doll cheaper and to be able to offer it to a larger market, I dispensed with the soft cloth as well as the production. It was an easier decision for me, because these hard dolls had a great success as well as a large market a decade ago; and so I gave my trust to produce this new doll in the hands of an old and well-known, leading doll manufacturer, that is the Rhenish Rubber and Celluloid Company, Mannheim-Neckarau. They offered, on account of their experience and 60 years of excellent reputation for quality products and progress due to new production methods, an absolute guarantee, that these new dolls would appear in a style which would leave no wish open and will awaken enthusiasm in the Children's World.

The understanding, with which my wishes, however difficult, were fulfilled and the love with which the gentlemen of this company went to work, appear to me to be a great omen for the future of this doll.

I beg you, to accept this new creation with warmth and joy. I believe in its success and hope that you will enjoy it. I wish everyone of us good luck on this new road.

Yours Käthe Kruse

beweglicher Kopf, Schlafaugen, lebensechtes Saran-Haar, Einzelkleidung
movable head, sleeping eyes, lifelike Saran-hair, individual dresses

Monika	*Susi*	*Gretel*
Hoch-Frisur	Kurzhaar-Frisur	Zopf-Frisur
Nr. 7 / 5994 / 40 / 102	**Nr. 7 / 5974 / 40 / 36**	**Nr. 7 / 5934 / 40 / 38**
DM 395,–	DM 395,–	DM 395,–

Gretel	*Gretel*	*Toni*
Zopf-Frisur	Zopf-Frisur	Kurzhaar-Frisur
Nr. 7 / 59144 / 40 / 37	**Nr. 7 / 59124 / 40 / 39**	**Nr. 7 / 5964 / / 40 / 1**
DM 375,–	DM 375,–	DM 345,–

Preise per 10 Stück brutto, Packung 1 Stück

Rotkäppchen
Zopf-Frisur
Nr. 7 / 5934 / 40 / 22
DM 375,–

Schallplatte
DM 25,–

Hans im Glück
Kurzhaar-Frisur
Nr. 7 / 5964 / 40 / 63
DM 345,–

Hänsel
Kurzhaar-Frisur
Nr. 7 / 5964 / 40 / 50
DM 295,–

Schallplatte
DM 25,–

Gretel
Zopf-Frisur
Nr. 7 / 5934 / 40 / 52
DM 345,–

Original pages from a 1961 Schildkröt-prospectus with celluloid dolls "Model Käthe Kruse". Especially interesting are the prices.

"Schummelchen"
Doll "45 H"

This doll appeared in 1956, measuring 45 cm (17³/₄ in) and having the same type of head as used for the former Doll I; this time, however, made of plastic, with a hand-knotted or braided real hair-wig.

This little body was a great novelty, as it was made of foam rubber foil modelled over a wire skeleton and covered with stockinet. The foam rubber alone represented the novelty as the wire skeleton had already been used for the "Little Soldier", "Schlenkerchen" and "Du Mein". "Schummelchen" was very flexible and could be made to assume countless different poses.

The catalogues from those days give the names "Scampolo", "Wickel", "Wackel", and "Biball". "Schummelchen" was signed on the right foot with the Käthe Kruse signature and number. The production of this doll ceased as early as 1957.

"Du Mein", Doll "50 BH"
(Baby with Hair) and with open eyes

As mentioned before, the doll "Du Mein" was allowed to keep her old name after 1950. But she was only manufactured measuring 50 cm (19³/₄ in), and nearly always with a whitish blond wig. Only very rarely, on special order, is she produced with painted hair or measuring 60 cm (23⁵/₈ in) (Doll VI). "Träumerchen" with closed eyes was and still is only made on order, almost exclusively for nursing purposes. She always has painted hair, an applied belly button and is weighted down with lead, so as to weigh 5 pounds.

"Du Mein" and "Träumerchen" were available until about 1965 with a magnesit head, whereas up to 1970 the body was manufactured according to the old wrapping system and covered with stockinet (see page 42). From then on until today, a plastic head was, and still is used. The body is made from formed and pressed foam-rubber plastic parts covered with stockinet; the arms are sewn on as on all Käthe-Kruse-Dolls. "Du Mein" is not weighted down and without a belly button. Signing: until 1958 with signature and number on the left foot, afterwards the signature was on the left foot and the date stamp on the right.

Doll "52 H" (formerly Doll VIII, "The German Child" with "Friedebald" head by Igor von Jakimow)

This traditional doll is represented, as always, measuring 52 cm (20¹/₂ in), but also after 1955, received a plastic head decorated with a hand-knotted real hair-wig. She is the only doll with one of the old types of heads to have kept her hand-stuffed muslin body until today. Her arms are sewn on, her legs fastened with disc-joints, the soles of her feet are strengthened with cardboard. From 1957 to 1969 doll "52 H" was not produced. Signing: until 1958 with signature and number on the left foot; later: signature on the left foot and date stamp on the right.

Doll "35 H" (former Doll Nr. IX, "The Little German Child" with a smaller "Friedebald" head by Igor von Jakimow)

Measuring 35 cm (13³/₄ in), this doll has been manufactured until today without any interruption; also, however, with a plastic head since 1955, whereas the body was stuffed in the old manner until 1977. The legs were fastened with disc-joints, and only after 1977 was the body made of formed, pressed and flaked foam-rubber plastic parts covered with stockinet. The arms are still sewn on, but the legs are screwed onto the body with a new mechanism in order to retain their mobility. This doll is also signed on the left foot with the Käthe Kruse signature and a date stamp on the right one.

Doll "35 BH" (Baby with hair)
The same doll "35" exists since 1956 also as a baby (see on the right) with hand stuffed muslin body and with floppy sewn on legs. As these little legs have a bridged foot sole, this doll could not be signed until 1982; she only wore the firm's well-known tag. From 1982 onwards, however, she has been stamped with the Käthe Kruse signature.

Doll "47 H" (created from Doll XII, "Hampelchen", until 1952 with floppy legs, now with disc-joints, standing firmly). Again the doll marking is identical with her size, 47 cm (18$^1/_2$ in). Doll "47 H" is now exclusively produced with a plastic head modelled by Igor von Jakimow. She is always fitted with a wig.
Until 1973 her body was made from hand-stuffed muslin. From 1973 onwards she has foam-rubber plastic bodyparts covered with stockinet, and movable screwed on legs. Doll "47 H" is signed on the left foot with the handwritten signature of Käthe Kruse; ten years ago the firm started to stamp the date on the same foot. She carries the firm's tag around her neck.

Doll "47 BH" (Baby with hair)
As a baby doll, doll "47 BH" always has a handstuffed muslin body and sewn on legs. Signing: none to start with, as the sole is bridged; from 1982 onwards, however, the Käthe Kruse signature is stamped on and the obligatory firm's tag added.

Above: "Doll 35 BH" with sewn-on legs. Below: "Doll 52 H" with ponytail (1950s).

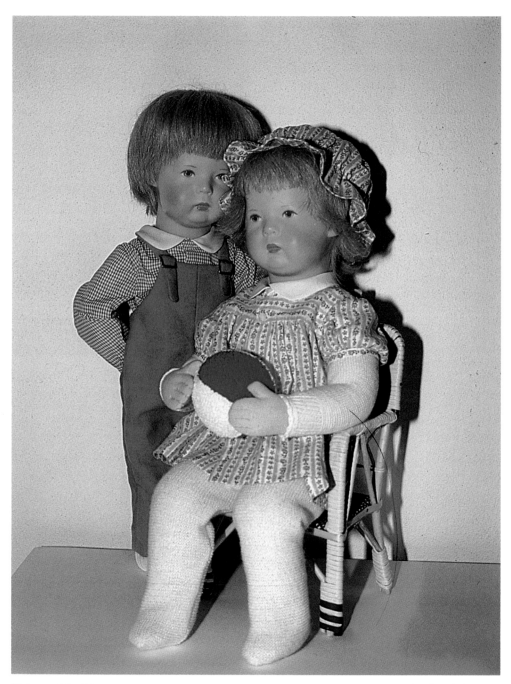

"Schummelchen" from 1956. Opposite page: two "Du Mein", 1983, synthetic head with and without hair.

78

Käthe-Kruse-Dolls: "Model Hanne Kruse"

Mrs. Adler-Kruse with her own doll creations "Graziella", "Däumlinchen", "Rumpumpel" and "Flessibila".

The third oldest Kruse daughter Hanne Adler-Kruse has substantially influenced the company development in Donauwörth since the 1950's. Above all, her doll creations brought new impulses into the enterprise. For the readers of this book, she wrote down in her own words how she came to design dolls, whether it was easy for her or not, which of her dolls were successful or had to be taken out of production again:

Sometimes I am asked how I conceived the ideas for my projects. This question is always connected with the strange idea that I somehow broodingly contemplate what I should do next and what it should look like. No, I make no "designs" and I do not contrive anything. To me, a design is something to be handed over to other people for their carrying it out; to people who prepare the design for execution. It is all very different with me. I have developed and completed each doll myself. In a way, I was never bothered by the thought of having to create something in order to achieve a higher turnover. Instead, I would rather say that the ideas developed from my work. I am delighted to tell you how my doll children came into existence in this way.

"Däumlinchen" was supposed to become a Christ Child for a calendar, nothing more than one single doll to be photographed. It didn't really need a face at all, one could have laid it into Mary's arms in such a way to only sense something of a little body being with her. In those days I had absolutely no idea that I was able to create something. I hadn't even worked with the company like my sister, and up to this moment had hardly any relationship with it. When I was a young girl, I attended an arts and crafts school, to learn how to model – only for one year, that was all. I even once modelled a male nude, but I was not really interested in all these modelling lessons. But when I started to model the little head for the Christ Child I discovered that something happened and was actually created. Nothing really dramatic happened but I could recognize something. And so I started carrying this little product around with me, everywhere I happened to be; so that nobody could possibly discover me over a job for which I was not given an order. And so it happened!

One does not produce a doll's head from clay and plaster. A reporter once wrote "one doesn't just sit in front of an easel and brood".

I worked without a design, without a sketch, and even without a precise concept; first the head, as far as I could model it with clay – my very first head was to be rather small. We must remember that the complete "Däumlinchen" is only 25 cm tall. Then a plaster mould was made, and the little plas-

ter head appearing in this way was filed. This filing is quite an important job because one can easily spoil the whole thing. I usually didn't manage it all with just one sitting and very often needed several moulds and repeated filings. But this is, after all, my own incapability, because I am not a sculptor and have neither training nor technique.

So finally came the day when the head was ready. I handed it over to the painting room, and I think it was first painted as a sleeping baby. But then it's eyes were opened and it received a wig. This was the moment when I forgot all about the Christ Child. I had a little skeleton made, took a foam-rubber foil and made a body pattern from several single parts which I glued together. Then I covered the little body with stockinet, put the head on, and all of a sudden it was a very sweet little girl doll.

That was it, and nobody was more surprised than I was. This happened around Christmas time and we took her with us for the first time to the Toy Trade Fair in early February 1957. And it was a great success. "Däumlinchen" was my greatest adventure.

Two dolls from the "Doggi" vinyl series, with the head of "Däumlinchen".

"Rumpumpel" which was born next, developed from the idea of making a baby doll. Up to then, we didn't have a baby doll at all amongst the play dolls. Our "Baby 35" had the "Friedebald" head which was

"Rumpumpel" doll, "Model Hanne Kruse".

not one of a very small child. I also wanted to have the limbs more babylike. I can't really say much more about this, only that I needed a long time to be able to recognize about the head: that is the best I can do, no better.

Altogether I must confess that this was always the point when I stopped doing something. Not because I thought it was perfect but because I couldn't do it any better. And nothing at all was ever easy for me. In spite of all this, I don't regard this artistic occupation as an achievement much that one may have trouble with it, but rather as a gift one receives. And there always seems to come the moment where one isn't the creator any more but where the relationship changes. That is, the creation takes over the lead and one's self is only the maker. Every artist may feel the same, if I may regard myself as such.

"Graziella": *I had the idea for "Graziella" when I spotted a jumping jack in a toy shop. I simply thought to myself "you can do that better". I didn't want to make a jumping jack but something that could be moved, nothing fidgety or jerky, rather something decorative. I liked this little wooden figure very much, but it didn't quite fit into our program of working with textiles, and so we decided to cease her production.*

"Graziella", a flat doll made out of wood and cloth, is very mobile.

"Flessibila": *A story in itself! The starting point was, that first of all I wanted a big doll which was fully articulated. I must have had the vision of my Mother's doll house dolls. As the wire skeleton for this could not be made from the old pattern, a very precious plastic skeleton was developed (I had already made the head for this some time ago). I had had the intention to make a soft doll "completely from cloth", covered with an extremely soft material. One was supposed to stroke the little face with the palm of one's hand, like one strokes a cat's head. Now that I'm writing all this down, I can hear my Father saying: "feelings come from touching" (I wonder whether this could be true?). I had some particular notions of tenderness for this one doll whose head was already modelled. This doll which I had named "mysterious being" to myself never got beyond an idea and was never made, but the covered head became available for "Flessibila".*

"Flessibila" was also rather nice; she could assume natural poses, and I still like her very much. But the skeleton never matured, nor did the body, really. Like "Däumlinchen", it was originally glued together from a single foam-rubber pattern and the manufacture was too complicated. So the production stopped. Without doubt "Flessibila" was the odd one out in our series and was not connected with Käthe-Kruse-Dolls any more.

My idea of a cloth doll still came true when some time later I created **"Mummelchen"** *which was to become our last born. I wanted to make a doll which lends itself to being dragged around by a toddler, which always looks pretty wherever she may be dropped or forgotten, which feels like cuddling, which can be taken to bed because her head is softer than our usual dolls; one which is more suitable for little children and easier in the manufacturing process. The use of a soft material for the so-called skin was due to the fact that our* machinery had been developed in the meantime to produce the forming and pressing of foam-rubber in such a way that the particular limbs did not have to be stuffed any more, like the classic Käthe-Kruse-Dolls. This process took place in reverse: the finished limbs were put inside the skin cover. The head is also formed and pressed. In some respect we had to renounce to our usual methods of production, much to our regret, yet our modern techniques opened new possibilities for us in many ways. However, we shall always aim to cherish and maintain the established and old, and be aware of our roots. Thus we shall never dispense with human labour and never move outside our garden but instead try to bring to it things that will thrive and prosper.

Hanne Adler-Kruse

Charming "Mummelchen", "Model Hanne Kruse", can be had with a bare backside.

In 1966, "Flessibila" was offered with three types of heads: left "Fessibila" head, in the middle with the head from Doll VIII and on the right from Doll I.

83

Description of Käthe-Kruse-Dolls, "Model Hanne Kruse"

With the introduction of these new dolls "Model Hanne Kruse", they were given individual names again, besides the markings of numbers and letters, such as "Däumlinchen", "Rumpumpel", "Flessibila", "Graziella", "Doggi", and "Mummelchen".

"Däumlinchen", "Model Hanne Kruse", 25 cm (9³/₄ in) – 1957

In 1957 "Däumlinchen" was introduced; a funny, bendable little doll measuring 25 cm (9³/₄ in) with a completely new turnable plastic head, modelled by Hanne Adler-Kruse. The immensely movable little body has a wire skeleton which was first glued over with shaped foam-rubber foil. Later this wire skeleton was formed and pressed into the body which was then covered with stockinet.

"Däumlinchen" soon became a great favourite and was manufactured in several versions:

- standing, with open painted eyes,
- from 1960 as a little negro with a frizzy real hair wig,
- as a baby with floppy legs and a wobbly little head (body from formed and pressed plastic, covered with stockinet),
- either open or closed painted eyes and painted hair if desired.

All standing "Däumlinchen" are available with hand-knotted real hair-wigs with a choice of blond, dark or red colour. From 1967 to 1982 they were also offered with painted hair. Today they are only available on special order in this version. All red-haired "Däumlinchen" have freckles and are particularly lovely. "Däumlinchen" feet are too small for signing so she has a tag with the Käthe Kruse signature sewn into her back and the firm's tag around her neck.

"Rumpumpel", "32 H and 32 BH" "Model Hanne Kruse", 32 cm (12⁵/₈ in) – 1959

"Rumpumpel" – 32 cm (12⁵/₈ in) – is the second small child amongst the Käthe-Kruse-Dolls modelled by Hanne Adler-Kruse and appeared on the market in 1959. She has a turnable plastic little head with a wig, but she could also be found with painted hair from 1967 to 1970. Her little body was and is always manufactured from muslin and handstuffed with reindeer hair. The legs are fastened with disc-joints. "Rumpumpel" also exists as a baby doll, also with a handstuffed muslin body but with floppy dangling legs. "Rumpumpel" as a toddler with straight legs is signed with the handwritten Käthe Kruse signature on the left foot. The right one has the date stamp. The baby doll was only signed from 1982 onwards.

"Flessibila", "Model Hanne Kruse", 49 cm (19¹/₄ in) – 1963 to 1968

Many collectors and lovers of Käthe-Kruse-Dolls will be surprised when they look at "Flessibila" – a creation by Hanne Adler-Kruse – for the very first time. She represents the absolute outsider amongst the very familiar doll children. While "Däumlinchen" and "Rumpumpel" fit harmoniously into the Kruse circle, "Flessibila" steps out of line completely, because she is such a super modern little soul. Her slightly stylized little face was a daring new venture.

"Flessibila" received a hand-painted plastic head with a braided or hand-knotted real hair-wig. Her body was glued together from foam-rubber parts and covered with stockinet. Heinz Adler had developed a plastic skeleton which enabled her to be

A group photograph with "Flessibila" (in the middle), ▷
and in front "Däumlinchen" with her black sister and on the right "Rumpumpel".

very flexible and to move just like a child. "Flessibila" was quite unique because she could be bought with a choice of three different heads (see page 83); namely Head I, Head VIII and head "Flessibila". But most buyers choose the usual old heads with the little faces they had grown fond of and therefore she was not a success; her production ceased.

Signing: as usual on the left foot; she wears the firm's tag around her neck.

"Graziella", "Model Hanne Kruse"
"Graziella" was produced from 1963 to 1967 and measured 47 cm (18½ in). She was a toy, wall decoration and painting

Original "Däumlinchen" tag from 1983.

model all in one and was made of flat wood. Her little head was decorated with cheerful woolen hair in beige, rusty red, yellow and orange and she possessed nearly unlimited movements. The catalogue from 1967 offered her in a blue silk dress or in a red dancing tunic, in a colourful striped frock or in rompers.

Signing: stamped on the back of the left foot with Käthe Kruse – "Model Hanne Kruse".

"Badebaby", Head "Model Hanne Kruse"
"Badebaby" appeared on the doll market in 1963 and was manufactured until 1974.

Her little head was that of the "Rumpumpel" doll, her body was supplied by the firm of Rheinische Gummi- and Celluloid-Fabrik (Schildkröt = Turtle). She was made from unbreakable plastic, and therefore very suitable for bathing.

Signing: "Badebaby" was not signed, it only carried the firm's tag.

"Doggi", "Model Hanne Kruse"
"Doggi's" doll life lasted from 1964 to 1967, she was 25 cm (9¾ in) tall and was a vinyl version of "Däumlinchen". The artificial hair was machine sewn onto the head.

Signing: "Doggi" had the signature of "Käthe Kruse" impressed on her back and wore the firm's tag around her neck.

Plush and Towelling Material
In 1967 a new branch of toys appeared in the Kruse works; toys made from towelling material and plush (see page 87). Amongst others, there are, for example, babies, balls and animals (teddy, duck, donkey) made from towelling material. From 1968 there were also animals and balls made from plush. Since 1974 there is the "Family Timmermann" made from towelling material, and the newest creation in 1981, "Mummelchen". Toys made from towelling material are not signed.

"Mummelchen"
"Mummelchen" is a baby measuring 36 cm (14⅛ in) and entirely made from formed and pressed plastic, covered with nicki material and equipped with a wig made from plush. It is the ideal toy for the toddler – soft, warm and cuddly, just right for loving care and for taking to bed. She is not signed, but she has a tag with the woven "Käthe Kruse" signature sewn into her back and the firm's tag around her neck.

Above: "Badebabys" taken from the 1969/70 company prospectus. Below left: "Family Timmermann", made out of towelling material. Below right: "Mum-melchen", 36 cm (14¹/₈ in), made from formed foamed-synthetics, company catalogue 1981/82.

Cheeky looking "Däumlinchen" with freckles; synthetic head, real hair-wig and her hands and feet are not made to detail. A lovely series of pictures of two "Däumlinchen" dolls, photographed by Mrs. Borgé, daughter of Mrs. Adler-Kruse.

88

89

Left: two "Rumpumpel" dolls as brother and sister; above: portrait of "Flessibila".

Dolls waiting to be mailed: "Who will become my doll mother?"

"Mummelchen" in her packing case waiting to be sent into the big world.

93

Käthe-Kruse-Workshops – today

In 1946, Donauwörth, became the second home for the Käthe-Kruse-Workshops. Thanks to the initiative of the Kruse sons Michael and Max the rebuilding of the business was undertaken immediately after the war. A refugee's fate may have struck Käthe Kruse very hard, yet she was fortunate enough to witness the continuation of her life's work in Donauwörth after 1950. Not only that, her vitality allowed her to participate actively in the firm, to undertake business trips and hold specialized expert lectures – up until a blessed old age. From 1958 onwards her third oldest daughter Johanna carried on the artistic side of the business, after a change in the management and enterprise. Her husband Heinz Adler steered the business into a new course of success. Paired with his wife's new doll creations, and his lucky hand in commercial and technical fields the Käthe-Kruse-Workshops blossomed again.

For the readers of this book, we decided to pay a visit to the second generation of the Kruse family, their workshops and all the doll children born there.

Arriving from Munich, just before the town of Donauwörth, one finds attractive and modern buildings on the work's own premises, at No. 9, Alte Augsburger Strasse. The workrooms are linked to the administration building, and it is here that the beautiful, much loved Käthe-Kruse-Dolls are created. But first of all one has to get over the shock of a confrontation with the manufacturing process. A basket with unfinished bodies is standing here, over there another one filled with plastic heads, and hundreds of little legs are dangling on the wall; painted doll heads are stuck for drying on wooden poles in a special drying room, in another room women busily stuff the bodies of particular doll types, traditionally with reindeer hair; and then, extremely modern, on the other side a large machine for the firm's own manufac-

ture of plastic parts. And then again a place for individualists and artists: the painting of eyes. One from the original staff and four other women paint with great skill the doll eyes and for certain types also the hair. Only here the mentioned shock begins to volatilize, here, where the doll starts to turn into a doll. But the great relief only comes with the visit to the assembling department where the dolls are put together, then with the visits to the impressive sewing rooms and the stylists of the real hair wigs: here they lie, sit, stand on tables and in baskets, and are ready to be dispatched from the mailing department. Bedded in boxes, printed with the proud signature "Käthe Kruse" they may now go out into the big wide world. And maybe, one of them will return to their place of birth to be healed from harm done by rough "child abuse".

After this general description of the workshops here are some technical facts which are of interest about the manufacture of dolls:

The pink-tinted first rough moulds made from plastic (Polystyrol) are polished and sprayed twice which gives them their proper complexion. The basic colour is painted on the mouth and eyes with a stencil to be then carefully completed by hand with a brush and oil colours.

The production of bodies is fundamentally different to the uniform production of heads. Doll bodies "52 H" and "32 H" as well as baby dolls "47 BH", "35 BH" and "32 BH" are made from muslin according to the original methods and handstuffed with reindeer hair. The arms are always sewn on, but the little legs on dolls "52 H" and "32 H" are fastened with disc-joints and splints, those of baby dolls "47 BH", "35 BH" and "32 BH" are sewn on.

Since 1973 formed and pressed foam-rubber plastic bodyparts were used, namely for "Träumerchen" and "Du Mein" as well as for dolls "47 H", "35 H" and for

"Däumlinchen". These bodyparts are thoroughly formed in an expensive process for a defined tightness and heaviness. As these parts have an extremely smooth surface and the cloth coverings should not slip around, they are coarsened afterwards by a flaking machine. This is done as follows: the bodyparts are covered by hand with glue, put onto an electrode and then into the flaking machine. Once inside, the flakes are drawn onto the limbs electrostatically, which only takes 20 seconds. The parts dry immediately. The bodyparts and heads for dolls "Du Mein", "Träumerchen" and "Däumlinchen" are knotted together with foamed and pressed strings and the ends stitched up. Then the stockinet, limb covers, fitted and partly sewn, are pulled over the limbs and the openings are tightly handsewn three times. The leg fastenings with dolls "47 H" and "35 H" are yet again different, in that they are screwed onto the torso after covering the legs with stockinet, by a new revolving-mechanism. Nuts are already formed and pressed into the plastic bodies, disc-joints and screws into the legs, so that the parts can be screwed together. This leaves the legs as movable as with dolls "52 H" and "32 H".

The standing "Däumlinchen" has a body foamed over a wire skeleton which is then covered with stockinet. "Mummelchen" has formed and pressed bodyparts covered with nicky material. On the other hand, the baby made from towelling material has impregnated foam-rubber foils which are die-cut by hand, sewn together and covered with towelling material.

To finish them, the dolls receive pretty, lavishly knotted real hair-wigs. The one and only Kruse doll with a mohair-plush-wig is "Mummelchen". Painted hair is now only to be found with "Däumlinchen-Baby" and on special order with "Du Mein" and "Träumerchen". The painting of hair is executed by a female painter who has been with the firm for 33 years. After all the described procedures the finished dolls are taken into the clothing department where they are given their wardrobe as stated in the catalogue. The extremely tasteful designs are mainly made by Hanne Adler-Kruse and her assistent, the colours being discreet yet vivid. The clothes are lovingly matched with the headgear and leather shoes. Quite clearly the trend of patterns moves more and more towards simplicity, corresponding with today's fashions. But there are also dresses for festive occasions, little coats, traditional costumes, nighties and pyjamas, knitted garments and sportswear. As in former years, mainly cottons, voile, cambric and wools are used.

Finally: the firm's premises has an area of 1500 square meters; there are about 80 employees within the firm, and 85 home-workers. All this makes the annual production of about 15,000 Käthe-Kruse-Dolls possible.

What happiness to realize that the tradition of Käthe-Kruse-Dolls is looked after and cherished.

Two "Rumpumpel", "Model Hanne Kruse", 32 cm (12⁵/₈ in) tall.

A visit to the Kruse-Workshop in Donauwörth: Heads, bodies and legs made out of synthetics waiting for further treatment, like polishing, painting, flaking and then completion, etc. Above left: The machine for producing synthetic parts, very important equipment for cheap production.

Above left: Cloth bodies, which are today still being stuffed by hand with reindeer hair. The following pictures show the sewing, painting and the assembly departments, where the legs are screwed into the bodies. Below: Marking out the body, combing of the wigs and the repair departments.

Friedebald Stories

experienced and told
by Sofie Rehbinder-Kruse

Friedebald and the little Donkey Rosinchen

My little brother Friedebald who learnt how to walk by hanging on to my plaits and who gained some popularity through the doll, made and named after him, grew into a lively, adventurous, and humorous lad. As the saying goes: he was the sunshine of our lives. With his imagination, warm heartedness, his cleverness and wealth of ideas he made our lives much livelier. I was his "much older sister". He was nine when I was twenty-three, and because he was raised mainly by me there always remained a certain mother-child relationship between us, and from this I thought I could derive the right and reason to continuously teach and train him.

I still remember wandering through the workshops, wearing my working pinafore, watching our seamstresses over their shoulders, working, when suddenly someone pulls at my frock and whispers "hey you, please give me some money!" I turn round, arrange his wild hair on his forehead and say: "Well now listen, it isn't as easy as that, simply "give me money". You are quite a big boy now, maybe you could try earning your own money with some kind of job?" He looks frowningly up at me for a long time, full of doubt, and doesn't think I'm being at all nice! But he disappears, and quite honestly I forget completely about him, until lunchbreak.

Then he came back to me. This time I am sitting down, so that our heads are level. Triumphantly proud, he stands in front of me, a little straddle-legged in his ancient pair of leather trousers, both hands in his pockets, rattling them like anything. "Listen, what do you think I have in here?" It is a strange noise and my guess is: pebbles. "No." He shakes his head. "Go on!" He would have loved to continue this guessing game but now it is me shaking my head: "I

Naked Friedebald learning how to walk using the plaits of his sister Fifi.

don't have time for long games, come on, show me!" He pulls his fists out of his pockets, slams them onto the table, opens them, and there in front of me are two heaps of copper coins. I, his sister, surprised and somewhat bewildered: "Where on earth did you get those?" "Well, didn't you say I should earn my own money? So I went to the refining works with Rosinchen and let the children have a ride, they enjoyed it thoroughly, and everyone had to pay me ten pfennigs, and I have to return immediately after lunch." (Do I have to explain that Rosinchen was our little sicilian donkey, especially ordered by Mother from Palermo for her doll deliveries. He came complete with a colourful two-wheeler cart and bridle decorated with feathers and glitter.)

Oh, I did like my brother's enterprise. It was the time of the summer holidays. Friedebald was occupied, he took his smaller brother Max with him, and the endless asking of what to do next had stopped.

But soon my well deserved peace also stopped. A few days later I am beckoned to the telephone – a slightly frightened young secretary saying: "Miss Fifi, the Lord Mayor!" It wasn't the Lord Mayor at all, just someone from the municipality, but was he strict! "Miss Kruse, do you happen to know that your brother has opened a business?" I retaliated. "Who, my brother Friedebald?" "Yes, the one with the fair curls and the leather trousers; but, you know, this is just not possible, he needs a licence for that, you have to apply for one first!" "Thank you for the information, I shall pass the message on to my brother, it will not happen again!"

Ah well; now all the boys were hanging around again, climbing trees in the orchard, disturbing chickens and ducks with their wild cries. Or they tried to escape me, only to play silly games by the river. In those few days I found no peace. But then I was called to the telephone again. It was that same voice, only this time asking in a shy way: "Oh, Miss Kruse, please allow your brother to go up to the works again, you cannot imagine the troubles we are having. All those mothers who come running and begging us to put an end to their offspring's pestering all day long, that they don't know what to do with themselves any more, and that they are fighting and simply intolerable, and all the mothers' chances for some peace and quiet have gone completely." "Well yes, but what about the licence?" "Oh, of course he doesn't need one, we would be so grateful if only he would continue."

The lost Umbrella

For my birthday I got an umbrella. Black, long and with a bent handle, as it used to be the fashion with umbrellas in those days. I got it from my brother Friedebald! Some time later I lost it, that is, I hadn't realized the loss, but it was pouring down, I had to be off, I was confused, when a surprised voice could be heard from the background, asking me "Why don't you use your umbrella?" I had to admit to not finding it, that I must have lost it. There was a long silence – then: "That is just typical of you womenfolk. We slave away to make you a present and you ..." During many a summer holiday Friedebald ran his business without any objection, and this helped him to attain a certain position of power; he was always followed by little boys and girls who depended on his goodwill for their donkey rides. He was not stupid; he recognized his chances! So he was always surrounded by a bunch of begging, hopping, and screaming kids.

Friedebald, donkey "Rosinchen" and his girl-friend Ilse.

Friedebald and his Girlfriend Ilse

As time went by there used to be a little blonde girl with Friedebald more and more often; she was allowed more and more rides, because she happened to be tired, because she happened to be so small, because she had knocked her little toe. More and more often he brought her home into the garden and looked after her, teased her, and was prepared to reach for the stars for her. Poor little brother Max became very neglected but there seems to be no cure for love. Was her name Ilse? I don't really know, Mother called her Baby, and for myself she turned into a sweet victim, clandestine and secretly, because in my never-ending search for different and nice heads she became a welcome model (page 106). The window manikin which thus was created, and called Ilse at home, became a real hit. This charming child simply lent herself to having a charming head made after her.

The umbrella, by the way, was found in the car one day, having been stuck between the back of the seat and the seat. Friedebald had to revise his verdict on women! His unusual name "Friedebald" (Friede = peace, bald = soon) was, incidentally, chosen because he was born just before armistice, on August 15, 1918. That he fell in Russia during the Second World War is a tragic stroke of fate we shall never forget.

Anyone who wanted a real hair-wig with his Käthe-Kruse-Doll had to send the real hair. The above letter from September 1949, shows this; this letter was sent by Käthe Kruse to her business friends.

1983 price-list, shows that the Käthe-Kruse-Dolls from today have their price as a well-made commodity.

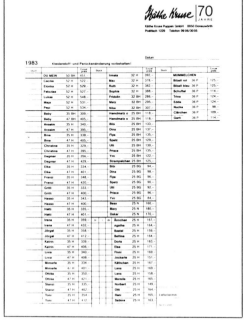

From left to right: Käthe-Kruse-Dolls with "Friede-bald" heads, with an unusual size of 45 cm (17³/₄in); Doll "35 H"; Doll "52 H"; Doll "47 H". All dolls have synthetic heads and hand-knotted real hair-wigs.

Käthe-Kruse-
Window-Manikins

There is only a very small gap to bridge in the development from a play doll into a figure for decoration. – At least this is what Käthe Kruse imagined when the department store Oberpollinger in Munich (Karstadt today) turned to her at the beginning of 1928 with the request to deliver dolls for a window display on Mother's Day, for ready-to-wear clothes in children sizes for three to five year olds. But she soon found out that this was much more difficult than she had at first expected. Many other criteria besides mobility and a firm standing pose had to be overcome. It took quite some time until the trials promised success, and so one continued to develop and perfect the project. It was most important to make the body movable by some inside apparatus. So a large metal skeleton was created, with the participation of a plumber who was engaged by daughter Sofie (Fifi), who herself played an important part in the realization of this whole project. This construction gave mobility and movability to the window-manikins unknown until then. They were later made in both, children's and adults' sizes.

The first head was made from the mould of her then three year old Friedebald's bust which Käthe Kruse had had modelled by her step son-in-law Igor von Jakimow. After this problem had been solved, it became most important to enhance the figure with even more charm and naturalness. This was achieved with a real human hair-wig. At the same time, this triggered off the idea to supply play dolls with hand-knotted real hair-wigs. This was practiced for the first time in 1929 on Doll VIII, the "German Child". – It was of course not possible to start a large range of window-manikins, with only one type of head. In the meantime, however, this became a target to be realized, as, automatically, more sizes were demanded. All of a sudden a variety of window-manikin heads were requested and thus daughter Sofie helped herself and started modelling heads. The result was so surprisingly excellent, even artistic, that it prompted her father spontaneously to remark that he had never experienced such a talent. It was obvious that daughter Sofie had inherited artistic talents from her father, the famous sculptor Max Kruse. It may be part of her fate that with her great talent she was never able to attend the academy but instead had to take on chores in their household and later on in the management of the firm. At the age of fourteen she started working as an apprentice in the Käthe-Kruse-Workshops, her mother's business, which was to keep her employed for nearly 35 years: as head clerk and manager. So even without studying she had a chance to develop her skills and to discover herself. She must have modelled about one hundred different heads for window-manikins after brothers, sisters, her own and other people's children, friends, acquaintances and famous people. A newspaper article of the time reported about the new window-manikins. "These movable window-manikins have become an attractive, artistic as well as advertising eye-catcher in shop windows, well beyond Germany's borders. The group of figures offered by Käthe Kruse in the German Pavilion during the Paris World Fair earned applause and admiration."

Just how uniquely beautiful these Käthe-Kruse-Window-Manikins were, is indicated by the following, extremely rare original photographs from the 1930's which certainly enriched this book a great deal. The production of window-manikins was continued after the war, since Käthe Kruse desired to spread their popularity. Only in 1962 was it decided to give up this part of the business.

The "movable window-manikins used for fashion and advertisement" are modelled individually by hand in that cellulose and gauze are covered over a wire skeleton. They are, due to their purposefulness, unbreakable and can be bent into any position.

The heads, as well as the wavy real hair-wigs, can be exchanged as well as replaced by new-ones, so that these figures are never out of fashion.

(All wigs are available in the colours blond, middle blond, chestnut brown and dark.)

The Normal Men's Model

for ready-made clothing with the suit measurements 44–50

Model 1, only sitting and lying, with all possible movements . . . . 510.– Reich Marks,

Model 2, only standing, in all various positions . . . . 525.– Reich Marks,

Model 3, the universal model, firmly adjustable, any position is possible,
  either standing, sitting or lying . . . . 575.– Reich Marks.

The Men's Model with Special Sizes

(our so-called dress figure)

Measurements according to request, 178–185 cm (70–73 in) tall, slim, with long legs,
for elegant tailoring, only delivered as a universal model . . . . 595.– Reich Marks.

Adolescent model, according to size and model . . . . 425–525.– Reich Marks

---

Stands for standing and universal models . . . . 3.50 Reich Marks.

Shoes and socks (size 42) are delivered by us at request, for the movable feet with the correct oval holes and are delivered at cost price.

The normal Women's Model

for ready-made clothing with measurements 38–42

Slender normal measurements in natural women's sizes, from head to foot 164–170 cm (65–67 in) (without measuring the heel), with heads Margarete and Marianne (at the moment), with nice daily hair-styles: low knot, neck bun, short curls, bobby hair etc. (hair-style group A), colour of hair at request:

Model 1, only lying and sitting possible, with all possible movements . . . . 450.– Reich Marks,

Model 2, only standing in all various positions . . . . 475.– Reich Marks,

Model 3, the universal model, firmly adjustable, any position is possible,
  either sitting, lying or standing . . . . 525.– Reich Marks.

If these models are wanted with fashionable evening hair-styles, large amounts of hair or special work (hair-style group B) – the price rises by 30.– Reich Marks.

Very new!   ## The Fashionable Model

for model clothing and pinning purposes

From head to foot, according to request, 172–183 cm (68–72 in), extremely long and slender, with long eye-lashes, rather fashionable make-up and with very modern hair-styles,
only delivered as a universal model . . . . 575.– Reich Marks.

Stand for standing and universal models . . . . 3.50 Reich Marks.

Shoes with high heels covered with black silk (or more elegant according to taste), as well as fashionable coloured stockings are supplied at request, with the right holes for the movable feet and are delivered at cost price.

Translation of the original text from the window-manikin catalogue of 1938.

"Mäcke" and "Roselind", two window-manikins playing with real kittens.

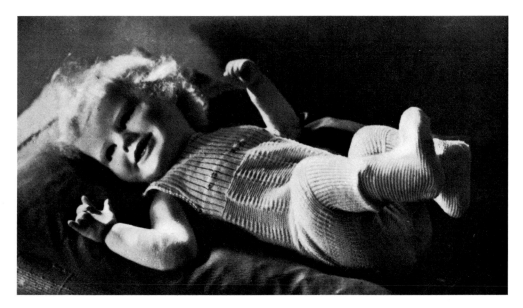

Above: The friendly window-manikin baby "Ambrosius", wearing rompers.

Below: Window-manikins "Philine" and "Ilse" with Käthe-Kruse-Doll prams designed by Jochen Kruse.

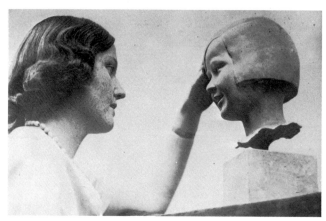

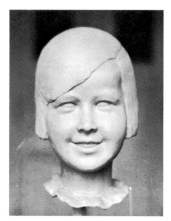

Above left: Friedebald teasing his girl friend Ilse.
Above right: A portrait of Ilse.
Below left: Sophie, nicknamed Fifi, modelling the bust of "Ilse". Next to this is the finished bust; compare with above picture.
Below right: This is the end product of a window-manikin "Ilse".

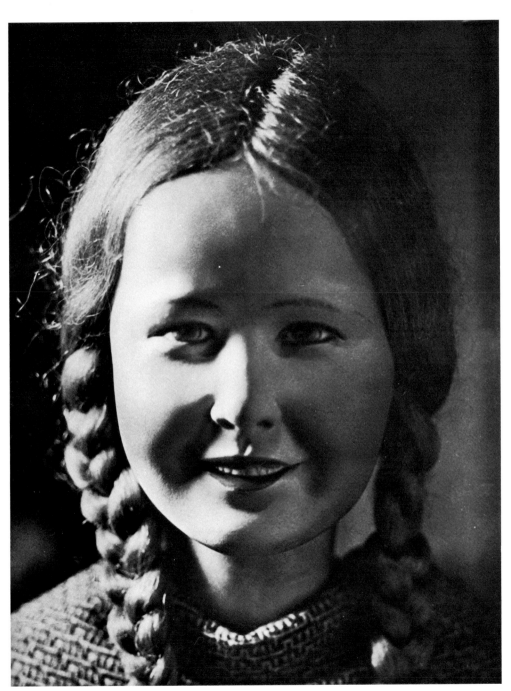

Portrait picture of the window-manikin "Ilse" with plaits.

107

Above: Two scenes of a wedding decoration at Oberpollinger (Karstadt) from 1928; below left: "Marietta" with "Friedebald"; right: Laundry day, notice the realistic poses.

Window-manikin "Margarete", modelled after the actress Liane Haid. All window-manikin heads, with exception of the "Friedebald" head, were made by Sofie Rehbinder-Kruse.

The Third Generation

The Changing of the Generations

Mrs. Hanne Adler-Kruse and her husband Heinz Adler successfully managed the Käthe Kruse Workshops until 1990. Due to their age, Hanne is 81 and her husband 74, and the disinterest of their children, they searched for a successor who would develop the valuable heritage further. Thus, on April 1st, 1990 the Workshop was handed over to Andrea and Stephen Christenson and the Family of the Prince zu Castell-Castell.

Andrea already played with Käthe Kruse dolls as a child, whereas her husband, an American who has been living in Germany for more than 10 years, came to love the dolls when coming to Germany. Both want to keep up this tradition and develop the valuable heritage further.

The high quality standards, traditional production and special focus on details are the most important attributes to be kept on in the future.

The Christensons want to address the different Käthe Kruse Doll lovers and collectors by launching special dolls.

The Käthe Kruse Classic Dolls

We want to relaunch old doll styles in limited editions for our very special doll lovers and collectors. Furthermore we will offer reprints of old Käthe Kruse books, postcards, posters and clothes for the old doll types i.e. Doll I. The first relaunch is a replica of Doll I (1911 - 1952) Jockerle und Margretchen. It is meant to be an Anniversary-Doll celebrating the Changing of the Generations.

Jockerle and Margretchen

Jockerle and Margretchen are a limited edition of only 500 copies. For almost 40 years the Doll I-head was not used by the Workshop. The doll bodies are stuffed with deer

Jockerle and Margretchen, 1990, Jubilee-Pair, in rememberance of the «Changing of the Generations».

hair and they are 47cm tall. The real-hair wigs are knotted by hand. The faces are hand painted and the material of the heads is a vinyl-composition. She wears a blue poker-dotted Dirndl, a hat with a blue ribbon and holds a little flower basket. Jockerle wears real leather pants that show fine stitching and a handknitted, mousegrey sweater. Jockerle is wearing dark brown Bavarian shoes, Margretchen, black ones. Their stockings are hand made.

Marienchen - the youngest member of the «Käthe Kruse Doll Family», 1990.

Marienchen

Marienchen is a little baby doll, available either as Du mein or Träumerchen. The latter's body weighs almost 6 lbs and has hand painted hair. Marienchen feels like a sweet little baby who wants to be cuddled and kissed. The head is made out of PVC-material. Mariechen is wearing a christening dress and comes in a little basket. Only 150 pieces are available each year. Until now, the heavy version was only available for mid-wives and nurses as a training aid. In the next years to come further doll-replicas in limited editions will be offered to collectors, however, tbe next one, for the 80th Anniversary of Käthe Kruse Dolls, remains still a secret.

«Here we are!», 1991 collection

The Käthe Kruse Dolls for Children

A child for a child - this was Käthe Kruse's message. We found out that about half of our doll-lovers are children in Germany, and we hope that also in other countries children still have the opportunity to play with them. When Käthe Kruse started to make dolls, this was 80 years ago, her dolls were only meant to be for children. She wanted her dolls to fulfill the following criteria:
- a child for a child, soft, cuddly and warm;
- my dolls are alive, because they are little infants that need to be hugged, loved and cared for;

- the secret of my dolls lies in their childlike and natural appearance, in their softness and also in their weight;
- these dolls are friends for a life time, they appeal to one's own feelings.

And this is still very true today. We receive plenty of mail every single day from our young doll lovers. They have asked us a lot of questions which have motivated us in reinforcing the clothing and accessories, i.e., satchels, lamps, toys and furniture for these dolls.

114

«What cake are you baking», Collection 1991

Hanne Adler-Kruse developed not only dolls, but also other toys that bring joy to the hearts of children. Mrs. Adler-Kruse developed animals in a simple style that stands in sharp contrast to the overly realistic presentation of many manufacturers. The plush and terry cloth animals of the Käthe Kruse Company are meant to stimulate the imagination of their playmates. The animals are easy to take care of, durable, and of the same high quality, that have made all our products known and loved through out the world.

Index

Drawing by P. Kleinschmidt